SPARK ISLAND

KS2 National Tests MATHS Learning Adventures

Contents

Introduction	2
Practice questions	
Place value	4
Number calculations	5
Properties of numbers and sequences	8
Fractions and percentages	10
Ratio and proportion	13
Negative numbers	14
Handling data	15
Probability	18
2D and 3D shapes	20
Position and direction	23
Perimeter and area	24
Angles	26
Symmetry and transformations	28
Units and measures	30
Practice test	33
Mental maths test	42
Sample test questions and answers	44
Answers to practice questions	46
Answers to practice test	48

Simon Greaves and Helen Greaves

Introduction

The National Tests

All pupils in Year 6 take National Tests in May. They are designed to be an objective assessment of the work covered from Year 3 up to Year 6 and the results of these, together with assessment by the teachers, give a clear picture of children's overall achievement.

In Maths there are three tests: Test A, Test B and a mental test. Children can't use a calculator in Test A or the mental test but they can in Test B. Children are allowed 45 minutes for Test A and 45 minutes for Test B. The mental test is a bit different and takes about 20 minutes. In the mental test the questions are read out on a tape and children have a few seconds to answer each question.

What is covered in the tests?

There are four main areas:

- Number – work on numbers and the number system, calculations and solving number problems
- Shape, space and measures – including 2D and 3D shapes, the position and movement of shapes and different measures
- Handling data – working with data and presenting information in different ways
- Learning how to apply mathematical skills and explaining the reasoning.

Topics can appear in any test. Most of the Key Stage 2 material will be tested but it is impossible for the tests to cover everything.

What are the questions like?

You will see from the practice questions section in this book (pages 4-32) that there are several different styles of question. These are some typical styles:

- A question with several 'tick box' or 'circle' answers where children are asked to tick a number of boxes or to circle things. They need to make sure they only tick or circle the number asked for. If they tick more they will lose marks.
- A question asking them to join lines between boxes, shapes or numbers. They should make sure the lines are clearly drawn but it's a good idea for children to complete the test in pencil so they can rub out any mistakes.
- A question asking for an explanation or reason. Children should explain their calculations using the correct vocabulary.
- A question with an answer box which asks children to show their working. These are worth two marks. Even if they get the wrong answer but show some correct working they may be given a mark.
- A question which needs special equipment. This could be a ruler or protractor for accurate measuring or drawing; a mirror or tracing paper for some shape questions.
- A question which uses a table, chart or graph. Children either need to complete it or get information from it.

Helping your child to prepare for the tests

Think about the best time for working. It might be easier at a weekend or early in the evening. Most of all, pick a quiet time when your child is eager to learn and not too tired. Find a suitable place where he or she can work comfortably without being disturbed, then make a start on the practice questions.

When you think you have revised all the topics, your child can try the practice test in this book. Mark it using the answers at the back of the book and then look at any wrong answers together. After some more revision your child can try the test again. Tell him or her not to be afraid to write their working or jottings on the paper itself. There's plenty of space for this. They aren't allowed to use scrap paper.

There are detailed answers for all of the practice questions. Make sure that you go through your child's incorrect answers and explain what he or she did wrong. Help him or her to work out what would have been a good answer.

There are detailed answers too for the practice test (marked out of 40) and the mental test (marked out of 20). You can use the scoring table (page 48) to work out an approximate level for your child's performance.

At the back of this book, there are some questions taken from recent National Maths Tests together with sample answers. These give some guidance on what makes a good and bad answer. These can be used to help explain the best way to answer test questions.

What will children feel like on the day of the tests?

If they have done some preparation they should feel confident and may even be looking forward to the challenge of the tests. Try not to make them over-confident so that they rush through the tests without reading the questions properly and make careless mistakes.

Even if they have done lots of work they may still feel nervous. Tell them to remember the work they have put in. It's all up there in their head so remind them to relax, take a few deep breaths and take their time. Once they've started they will probably feel more confident.

How will I find out how my child has done?

The tests are sent away to be marked. The school will get the scores around the start of July. The teacher will then tell your child his or her level and you will receive a report.

Place value 9742

Bright sparks!

- When you are rounding numbers, look at the digit after the digit to which the number is to be rounded. If it's four or less then round the number down; if it's five or more then round it up.

1 Here are four digits. **8** **4** **9** **1**

(a) What is the **largest number** you can make using all four digits? ☐

(b) What is the number, nearest in value to **2000**, you can make using all four digits? ☐

2 Circle the number which is **closest** in value to **0·5**.

0·05 0·55 0·6 0·06 0·49

3 Write the number **4308** in words.

....

4 Here is a number line.

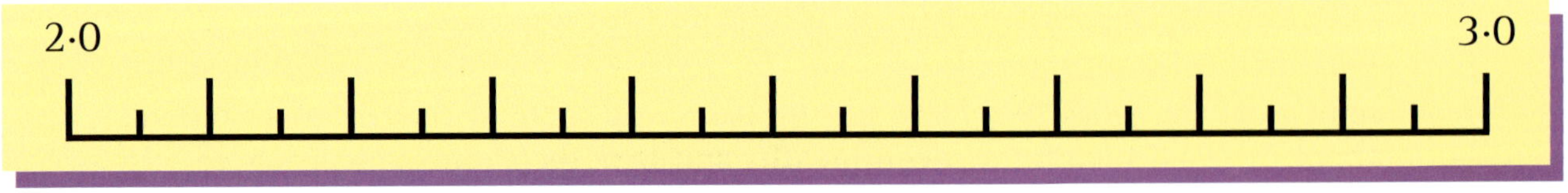

Draw an arrow ↓ to show the position of **2·45**.

Remember

> means greater than

< means less than

5 Write either > or < in the boxes to make each statement correct.

136 ☐ 160 1121 ☐ 1112 0·02 ☐ 0·1

Number calculations

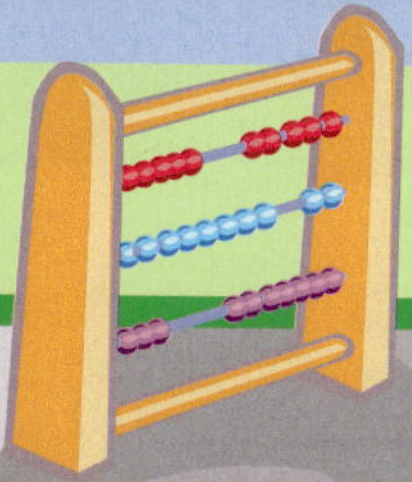

Bright sparks!

- Addition is the inverse of subtraction.
- Multiplication is the inverse of division.
- Other words for:
  add – sum, total, plus
  subtract – difference, take away, minus
  multiply – find product, times
  divide – find quotient

(*No calculator allowed for questions 1-9.*)

Show your **working**. You may get a mark.

1 Write the missing number.

☐ x 7 = 420

2 Calculate 942 ÷ 6. ☐

3 Calculate 15·36 - 9·52. ☐

4 Write two three-digit numbers which have a **difference of** 99.

☐☐☐ - ☐☐☐ = 99

5 Draw lines to join the calculations which have the same answers.

8 x 8	
9 x 7	45 + 18
Double 32	(5 x 9) + 8
99 - 46	

6 Write the missing number.

☐ - (35 ÷ 5) = 5

7(a) Jackson is given **£3.50** pocket money each week.

After how many weeks will he have enough to buy a CD costing **£15**?

(b) Lewis gets **20%** more pocket money a week than Jackson.

How much pocket money does Lewis get? £

8(a) Here are the costs of making phone calls to different countries.

Country	Price per minute
USA	10p
France	6p
India	14p
Turkey	7p

How much would a **nine** minute phone call **to India** cost? £

Show your **working**. You may get a mark.

(b) Callum phoned his uncle in **France**.
His call cost **72p**.

How many minutes long was his call?

9 Jessica is sending **three** parcels.

£1.60 85p £1.95

A B C

(a) How much more does it cost to send parcel A than parcel B? £

(b) What is the **total cost** of sending all **three** parcels? £

(You may use a calculator for questions 10–14.)

10 Write the missing number. 32 + ______ + 140 = 220

11 Here are some digits.

7 **5** **6** **9**

Use the digits in the sum to make the **highest possible** answer.

□□ + □□ = ______

12 Write three **single digit** numbers to complete the calculation.

□ x □ x □ = 245

13 Alisha has **£24** to spend on footballs and cricket balls.

(a) She must buy **five** footballs.

How much does this cost? £

(b) How much money does she have left? £

(c) She spends the rest of the money on cricket balls.

How many cricket balls can she buy?

14 Fill in the missing numbers so that each side of the triangle has a **total of 500**.

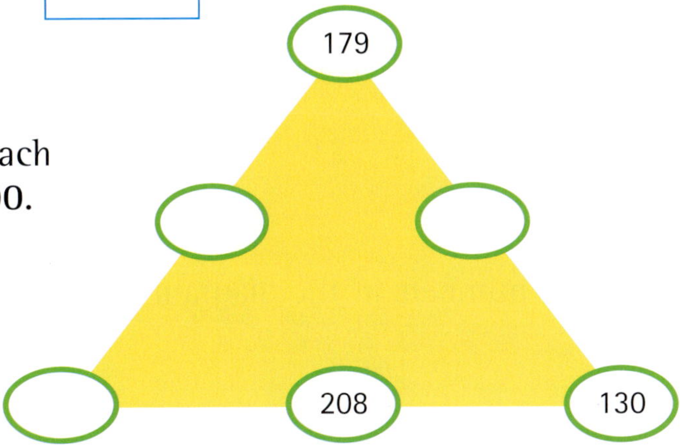

Properties of numbers and sequences

Bright sparks!

- **Multiples** are answers to your times tables.
- **Factors** are numbers that divide exactly into other numbers.
- A **prime number** is one which only divides by one and itself.
- A **sequence** is a list of numbers which are linked by a rule.

1 Here is a diagram for sorting numbers.

Write these numbers in the correct boxes.

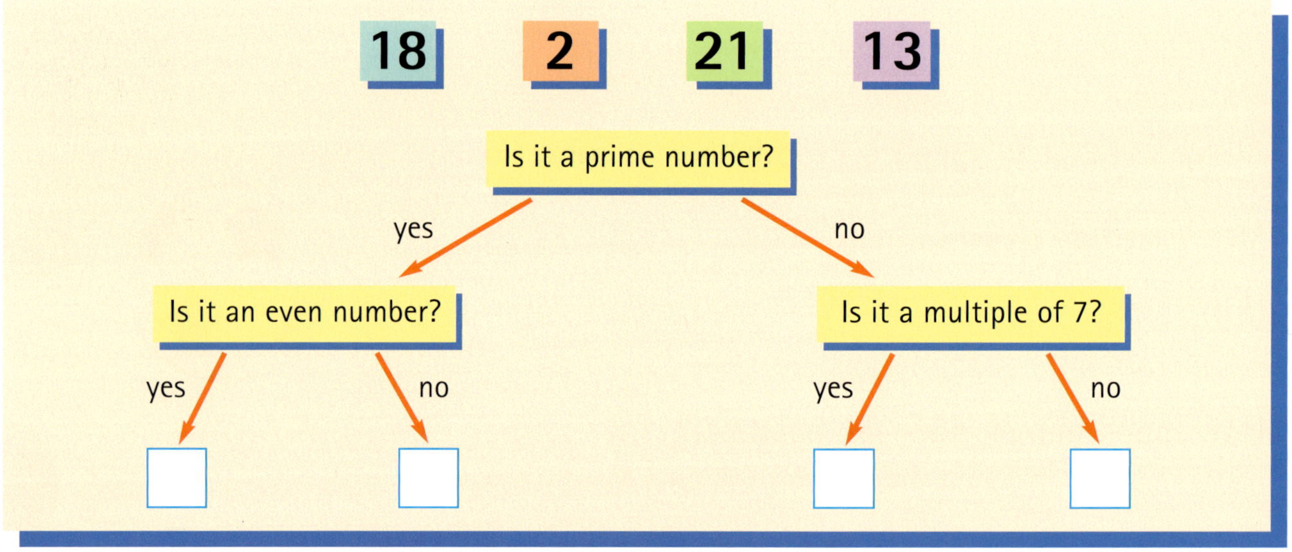

2(a) Here is a Venn diagram. It shows some numbers.

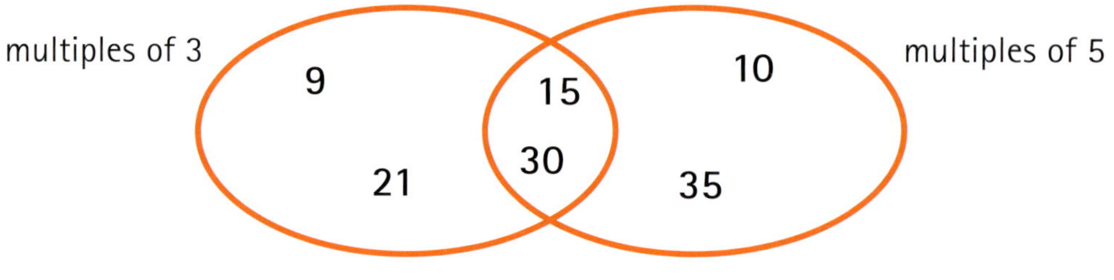

List **all** the numbers in the diagram which are **multiples of 3**.

....

(b) Here are some statements about the numbers in the diagram on page 8.
One of the statements is **false**.

Put a tick in the box next to the **false** statement.

9 is a multiple of 3 but not 5	☐	30 and 35 are both multiples of 5	☐
35 is a multiple of both 3 and 5	☐	3 and 5 are factors of 15	☐

(c) Find a number greater than 100 which is also a multiple of 3 and 5. ☐

3 The first number in a sequence is 13.
4 is subtracted each time to get the next number.

13 → 9 → 5 → ☐ → ☐

Write the next two numbers in the sequence in the boxes.

4(a) The rule for this sequence of numbers is **add on 60.**

300 360 420 480 . . . . . .

The sequence continues in the same way.

Write down the first number in the sequence which will be **greater than 700.** ☐

(b) Claire says, **'The number 3800 will not be in the sequence.'**

Is Claire correct? Circle Yes or No. **Yes / No**

Explain your answer.

....

....

5 Simon is counting in **equal steps.**
He starts at 33 and counts on two more numbers before getting to 51.

Complete the missing numbers. **33** → ☐ → ☐ → **51**

Fractions and percentages

Bright sparks!

- one whole = 100% = 1·0
- one half = 50% = 0·5
- one quarter = 25% = 0·25
- three quarters = 75% = 0·75
- one tenth = 10% = 0·1

- **Percentage** means the number of parts in every one hundred.
- An **improper fraction** has a numerator (top) which is bigger than the denominator (bottom).
- A **mixed number** is made up of a whole number and a fraction.
- **Equivalent fractions** are equal in size.

1 $\frac{3}{8}$ $\frac{4}{5}$ $\frac{1}{5}$ $\frac{3}{4}$

Write these fractions in order starting with the smallest.

☐ ☐ ☐ ☐

Show your **working**. You may get a mark.

2 $\frac{4}{7}$ of a class of 35 are boys.

How many are girls? ☐

3 Kate cuts a piece of string into two pieces.

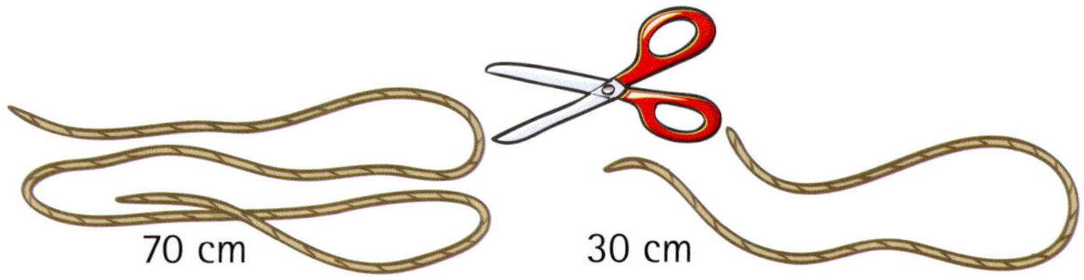

What fraction of the total length is the **shorter** piece? ☐

4 Here are three weights.

What is the total of the three weights? ☐ kg

5 Here are four digit cards.

8 **5** **1** **4**

Choose **two** cards to complete the statements.

$$\frac{\square}{\square} = \frac{1}{2} \qquad \frac{\square}{\square} < \frac{1}{7}$$

6 Here are some shapes.

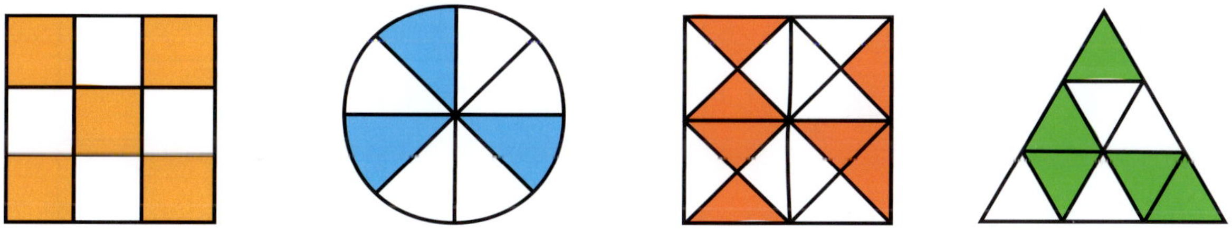

☐ ☐ ☐ ☐

Tick the boxes for the **two** shapes which are **more than half** shaded.

7 Find **two** different ways to divide the rectangle into quarters.
Each quarter must be made up of whole squares.

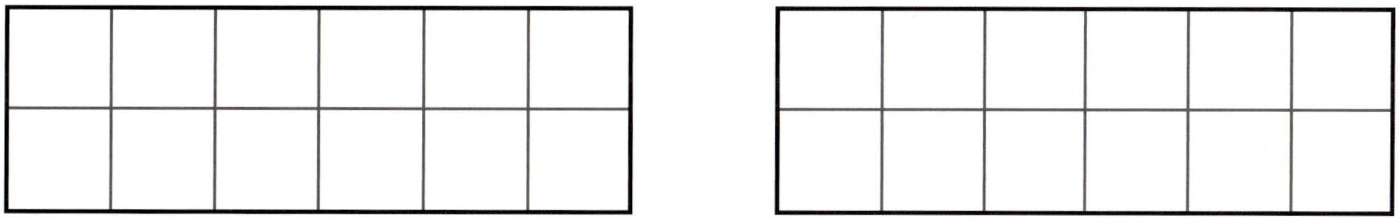

8 The table shows the fares for the number 15 tube to the Sparkanon.

Tube 15

Spark Harbour	–	Zoo	40p
Spark Harbour	–	Library	60p
Spark Harbour	–	Museum	80p
Spark Harbour	–	Sparkanon	£1.20p

The Elders have increased all fares by **10%**.

Work out the new prices.
One has been done for you.

Tube 15 *Increased Fares*

Spark Harbour	–	Zoo	44p
Spark Harbour	–	Library	______
Spark Harbour	–	Museum	______
Spark Harbour	–	Sparkanon	______

9 Here is a grid made of squares.

Shade **60%** of the grid.

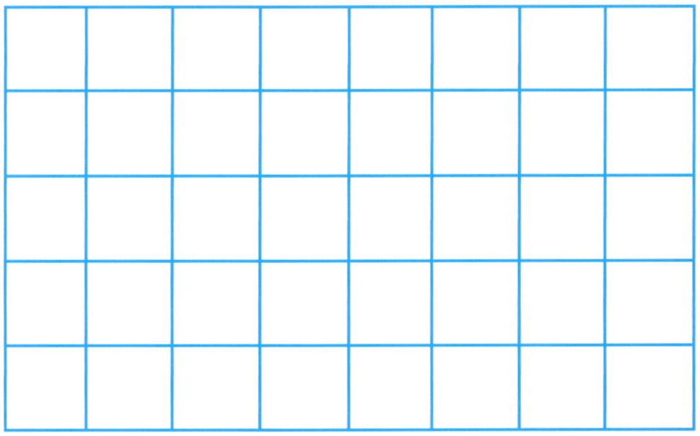

Show your **working**.
You may get a mark.

10 There are **240** pupils in Asif's school.

(a) **42%** are **boys**.

What percentage of the pupils are **girls**? [ ]

(b) **40%** of pupils in Asif's class are **boys**.

There are **12 boys** in Asif's class.

How many **pupils** are in Asif's class? [ ]

Ratio and proportion

Bright sparks!

- A **ratio** compares one part with another.
- A **proportion** compares an amount to the whole.

150 grams flour
100 grams butter
50 grams sugar

Makes 10 biscuits

1(a) Here is a recipe for biscuits.

How much **sugar** will be needed to make **15** biscuits?

[ ] grams

(b) Kim says, **'The ratio of sugar to butter is 1:2'.**

Is she correct?

Circle Yes or No. **Yes / No**

Explain your answer.

....

....

2 Ben has noticed an offer at his local supermarket.

Buy 5 packets of crisps and get 2 extra packets FREE

Ben buys some crisps.
He leaves the supermarket with **35 packets** of crisps.

How many of these packets were free? [ ]

Negative numbers

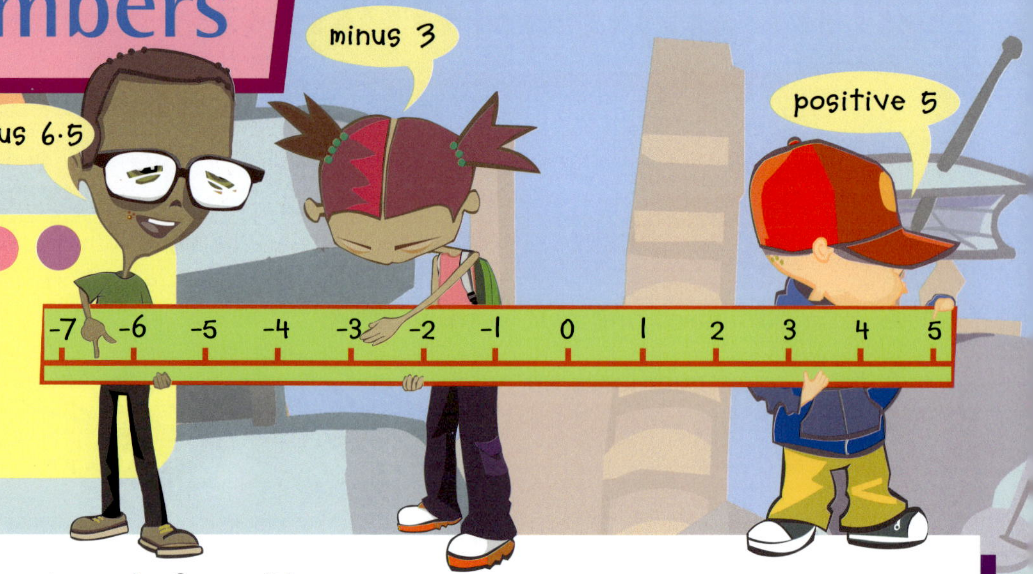

Bright sparks!

- Negative numbers are used in everyday life, for example, for temperatures, heights, money and coordinates.

1(a) The boxes show the temperatures in four cities.

London	Moscow	Madrid	Sydney
8°C	-3°C	12°C	22°C

Which is the warmest city? ☐

(b) What is the difference in the temperature between **Moscow** and **London**? ☐ °C

2 Circle the two numbers which have a **difference of 4**.

-6 -3 0 1 3 8

3(a) Sacha checks the temperature every hour on one day in January.

She records her results in a table.

What is the rise in temperature between **7 am** and **10 am**? ☐ °C

Time	Temperature (°C)
7 am	-3
8 am	-1
9 am	0
10 am	4
11 am	7
12 noon	9
1 pm	10
2 pm	10

(b) The temperature at 6 am was 2°C **colder** than at 7 am.

What was the temperature at **6 am**? ☐ °C

Handling data

Bright sparks!

- The **mode** is the most common number in a list.
- The **median** is the middle number in a list when all of the numbers are put in order.
- The **mean** is found by adding up all the values and dividing the total by the number of values.
- Data may be displayed in pictograms, bar charts, bar line charts, line graphs, pie charts, tally charts and tables.

1 This **bar chart** shows how many packets of crisps were sold in the school shop.

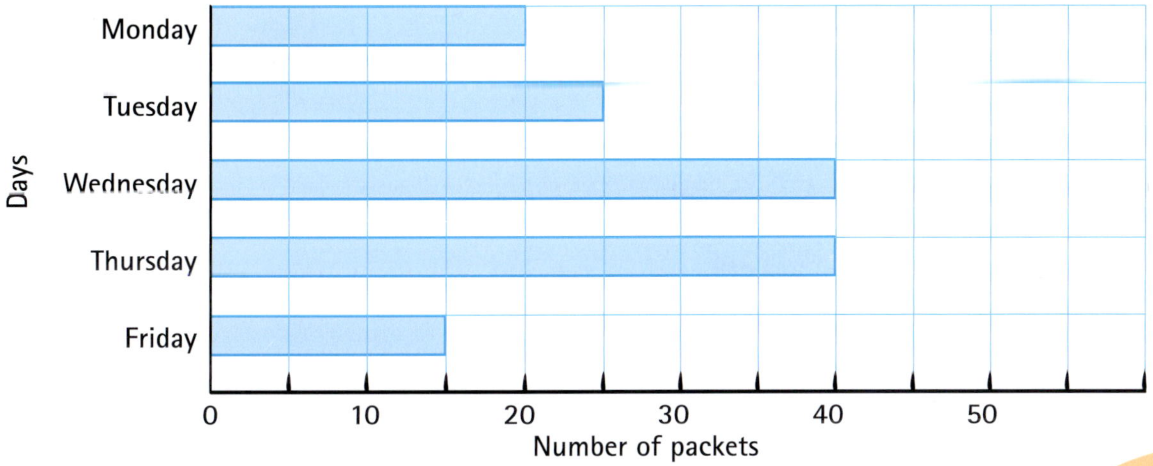

(a) How many packets were sold on **Tuesday**?

(b) How many **more** packets were sold on **Thursday** than on **Friday**?

(c) A packet of crisps costs **32p**.
How much money was made selling crisps that week?

(*You may use a calculator for this question.*)

£

Show your **working**. You may get a mark.

2 Here is a table showing the items in five children's pencil cases.

	pencil	ruler	rubber	pen	sharpener
Liam	✓	✓		✓	
Zoe	✓	✓	✓	✓	
Paul		✓		✓	
Jez	✓	✓	✓		✓
Danny	✓	✓			

(a) Which item do all five children have?

(b) How many children have both a **rubber and a pen**?

3 The pie chart shows the instruments played by **40** children.

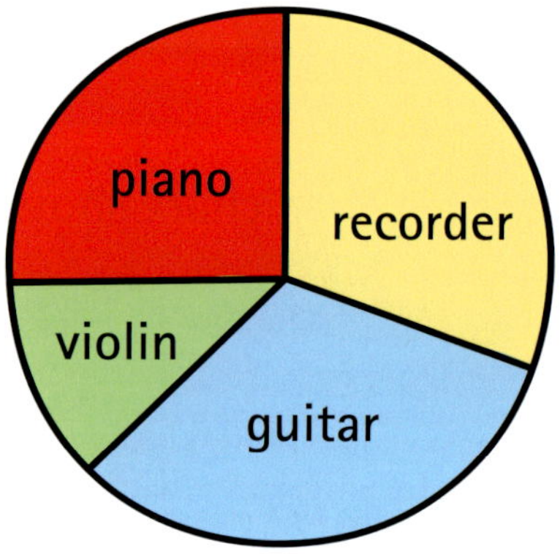

Estimate the number of children who play the recorder.

4 Kelvin cycled to the beach from his home.

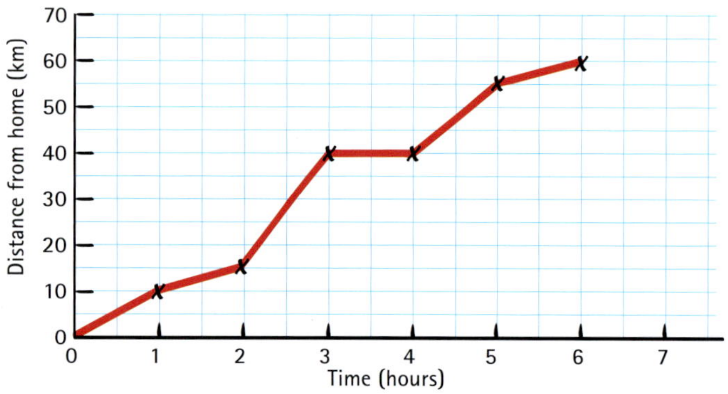

(a) How far is the beach from his home? kilometres

(b) How long did it take him to travel the **first 15** kilometres?

(c) What happened **between** 3 and 4 hours? Explain how you know.

5 The Spark Island football team has played twelve matches.

Zeb has recorded the number of goals the team scored in each match.

0	4	1	3	2	0
5	2	2	2	0	3

(a) Put the data into this tally chart.

Goals scored	Tally	Frequency
0		
1		
2		
3		
4		
5		

(b) What is the **mode** for the number of goals scored?

(c) Work out the **mean** number of goals scored.

Show your **working**. You may get a mark.

Probability

Bright sparks!

- **Probability** is a measure of how likely something is to happen. All probabilities are between 0 (impossible) and 1 (certain).

1(a) The spinner below is divided into six equal sections.

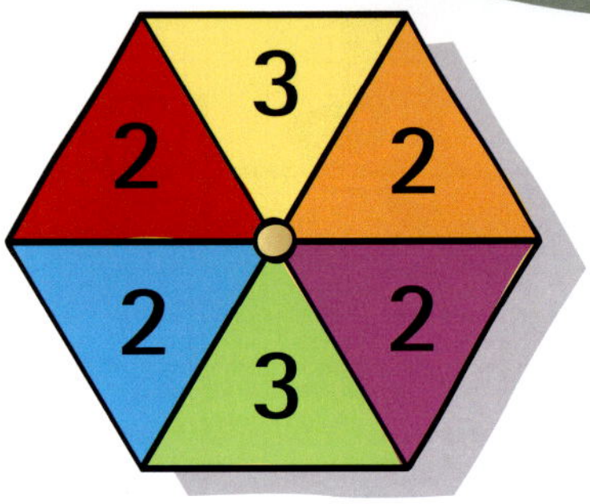

Keely says, **'There is an even chance of scoring a 2 or a 3 on the spinner'.**

Explain why she cannot be correct.

....

....

....

(b) What is the probability of landing on the number 2? ☐

(c) Keely is making a spinner.
She has started to write numbers on it.

Keely wants her spinner to be most likely to land on a score of 4.

Fill the rest of the sections with numbers so that it is most likely to land on a score of 4.

2(a) Twelve coloured cubes are placed into a bag.
There are three blue cubes, six green cubes, two yellow cubes and one white cube.

Asim puts his hand into the bag and picks out a white cube.

What is the probability of picking a **white cube** from the bag?

(b) Asim puts the white cube back into the bag and picks out another cube.

What is the probability that Asim will pick out a **green cube**?

3(a) Sarah is investigating all the possible totals of rolling two six-sided dice.

Here is a table which shows all the possible totals when the score on each dice is added together.

0	1	2	3	4	5	6
1	2	3	4	5	6	7
2	3	4	5	6	7	8
3	4	5	6	7	8	9
4	5	6	7	8	9	10
5	6	7	8	9	10	11
6	7	8	9	10	11	12

Which score is Sarah **most likely** to get?

(b) Explain your answer.

(c) Which two scores is Sarah **least likely** to get?

2D and 3D shapes

Bright sparks!

- **Triangles** have 3 sides – different types are **scalene**, **equilateral**, **isosceles** and **right-angled**.
- **Quadrilaterals** have 4 sides – special ones are **square**, **rectangle**, **rhombus**, **parallelogram**, **trapezium**, **kite**.
- A **pentagon** has 5 sides, a **hexagon** 6 sides, a **heptagon** 7 sides, and an **octagon** 8 sides.
- **3D shapes** have edges, faces and vertices (corners). If a 3D shape is unfolded and laid flat this is called a **net**.

1 Here is a **cuboid**.

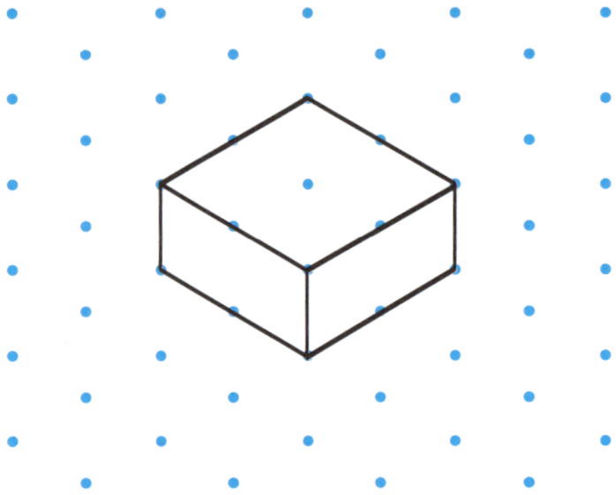

Complete the cuboid so it is **twice** as **long**, **twice** as **wide** and **twice** as **high** as the cuboid in the picture above.

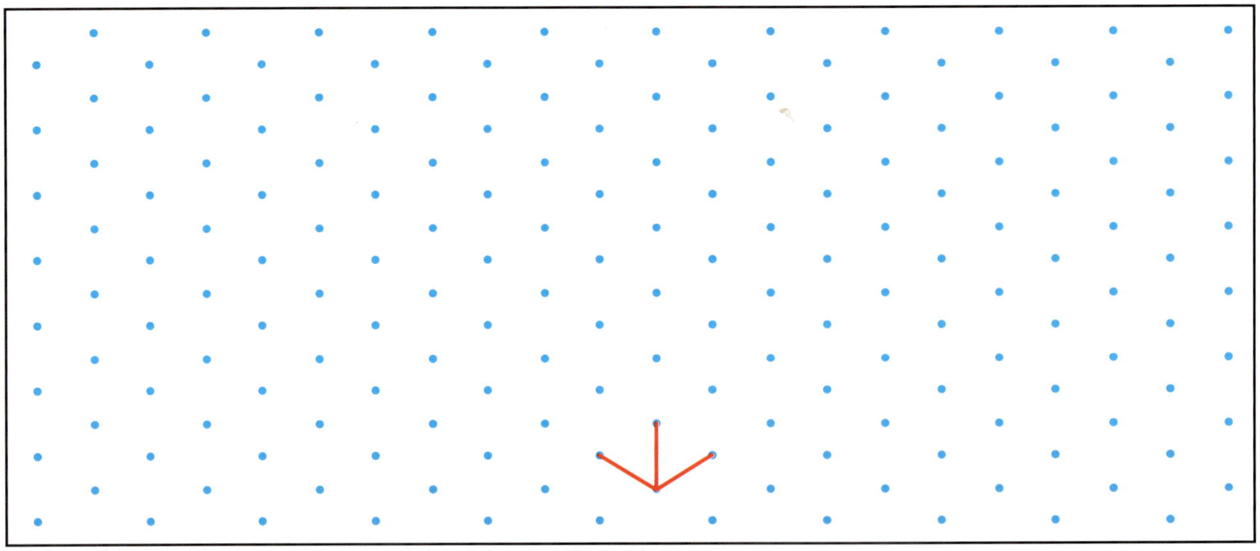

2 Here are some 3D shapes.

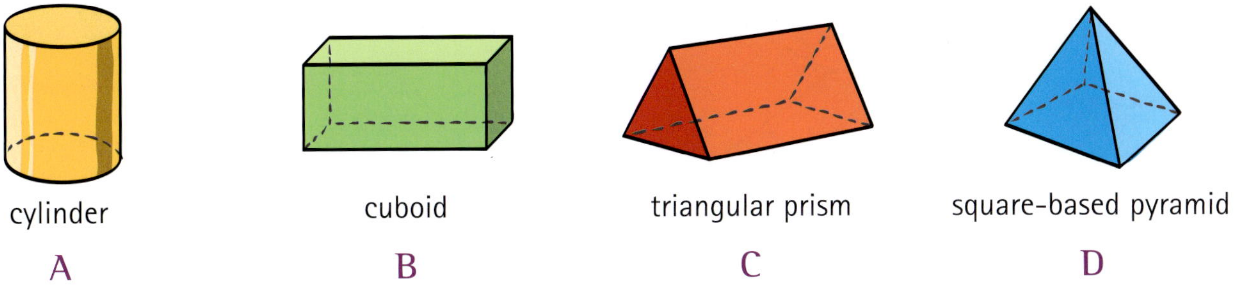

Write the letter of the shape which has **six vertices.** ☐

Write the letter of the shape which has **three faces.** ☐

3 Here is an open box.
It has a **square base.**

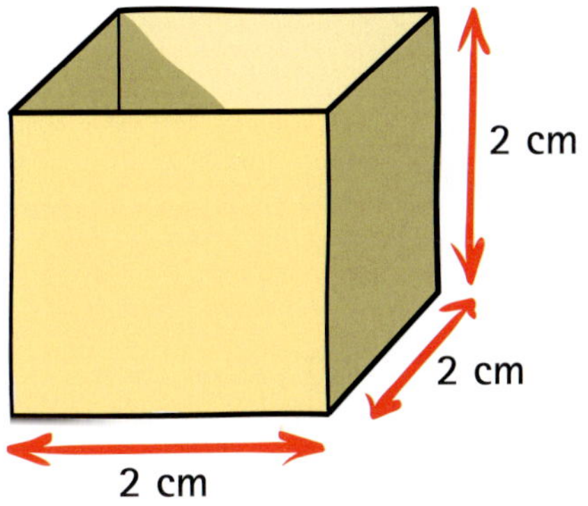

not to scale

Draw accurately the net of the open box in the grid below.

4 Look at the shapes below.

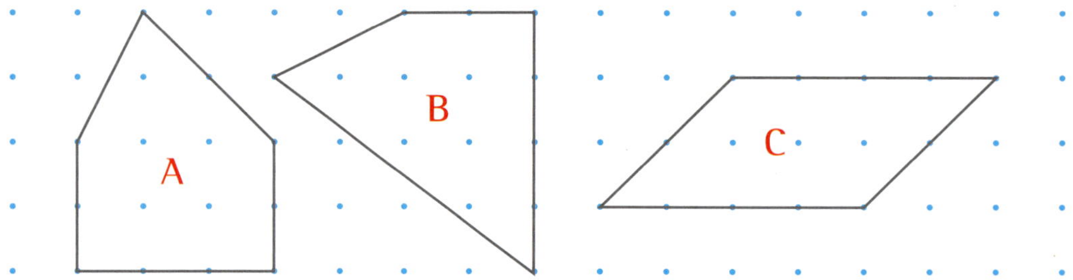

Write the letters **A** and **B** in the table below to show where they should go. Shape **C** has been done for you.

	4 sides	more than 4 sides
no parallel sides		
one pair of parallel sides		
two pairs of parallel sides	C	

5 One of the shapes below is a **scalene triangle.**

(a) Put a tick inside the scalene triangle.

(b) Which statement below best describes an **isosceles triangle**?

Tick **one** box.

☐ An isosceles triangle has three sides of different lengths.

☐ An isosceles triangle has three sides of equal length.

☐ An isosceles triangle has two sides of equal length.

☐ An isosceles triangle has three different-sized angles.

Position and direction

Bright sparks!

- **To plot coordinates** first go across, then up or down (along the corridor, up the stairs!)
- **Parallel lines** are always the same distance apart – like train tracks!
- **Perpendicular lines** cross each other at right angles.

1 Put a cross on the line that is **perpendicular** to the **line** AE.

What are the coordinates of D? (☐ , ☐)

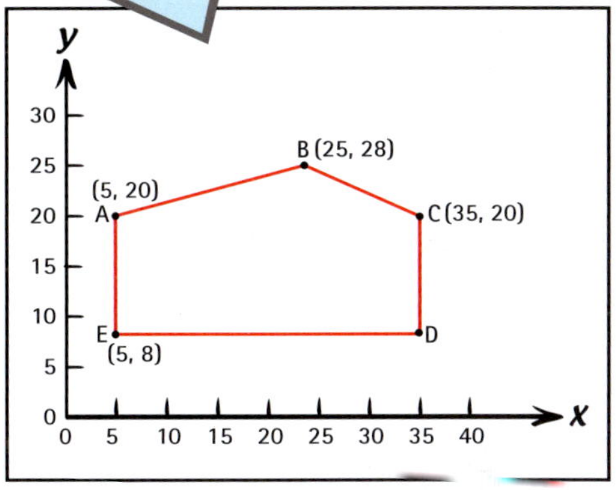

2 Here is a map showing some towns.

Which town is **north east** of Denham?

☐

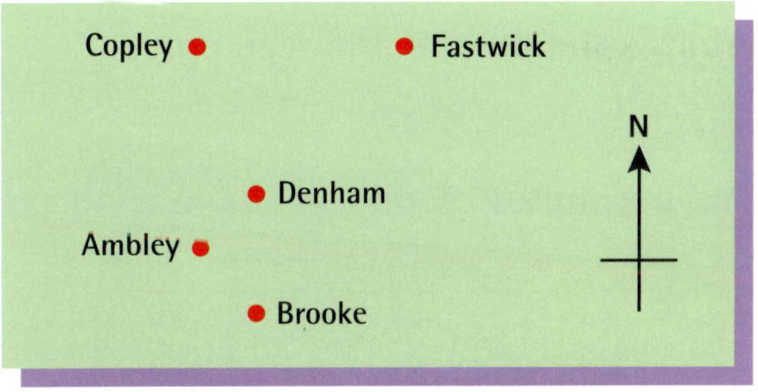

3 Sam has drawn a letter T on a grid.
It has one line of symmetry.
The vertical part of the letter T is 8 units long.

What are the coordinates of the point marked P? (☐ , ☐)

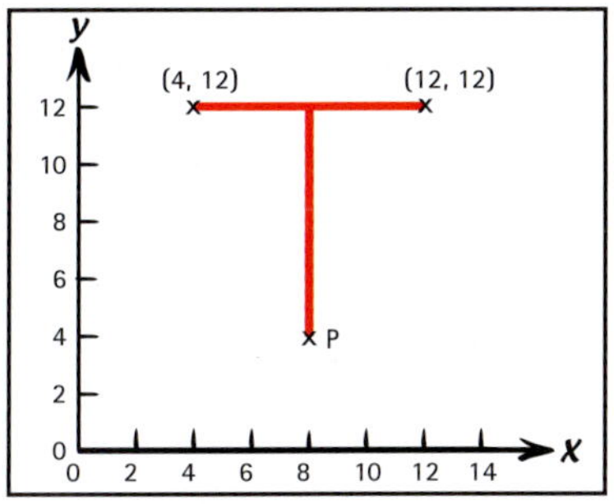

Perimeter and area

Bright sparks!

- **Perimeter** is the distance around the outside of a shape.
- **Area** is the amount of space covered by a shape.

1 Draw **two** more lines on the grid to make a quadrilateral with an area of 8 cm^2.

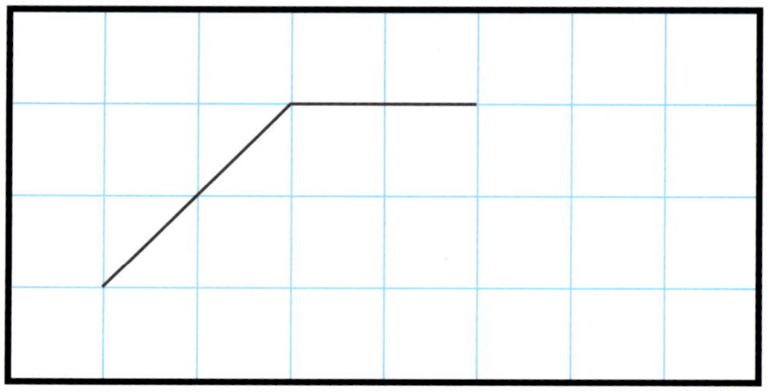

2(a) Leanne has drawn a rectangle.
The longest side is **12 cm**. The shortest is **4 cm**.

What is the **perimeter** of the rectangle? ______ cm

(b) What is the **area** of the rectangle? ______ cm^2

3 The **perimeter** of this rectangle is **48 cm**.

not to scale

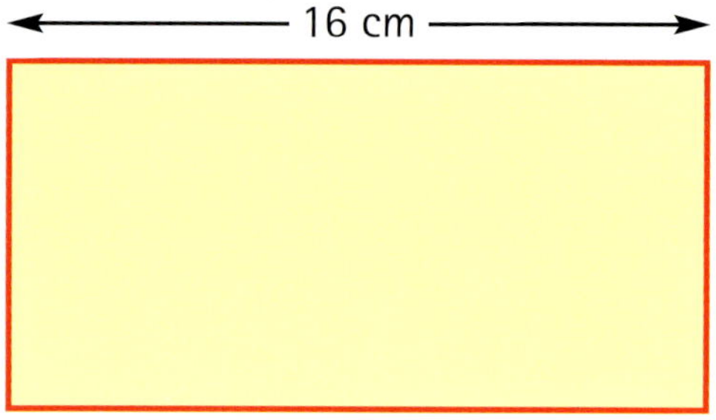

The length of the rectangle is 16 cm.

Work out the length of the **shortest side**.

______ cm

Show your **working**.
You may get a mark.

4 What is the approximate area of the shape in the grid?

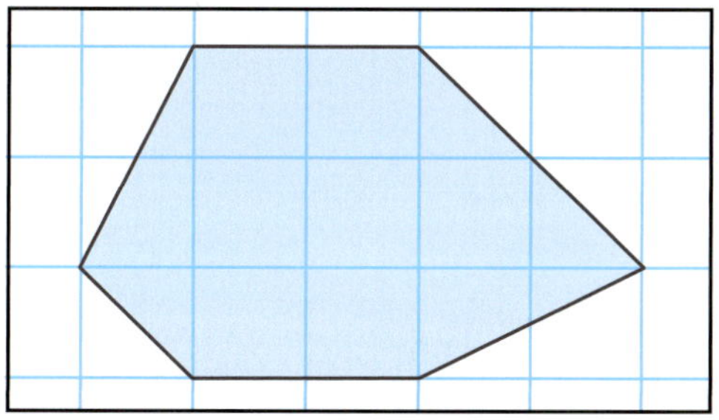

[cm^2]

5 Jason is making shapes with equilateral triangles like this one.

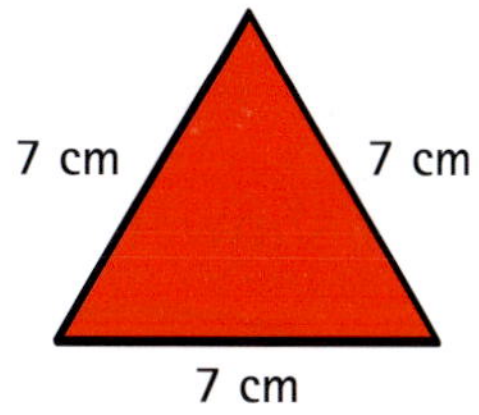

not to scale

He makes this hexagon.

What is the **perimeter** of the hexagon? [cm]

6 On the grid draw a **square** which has the **same area** as the shaded shape.

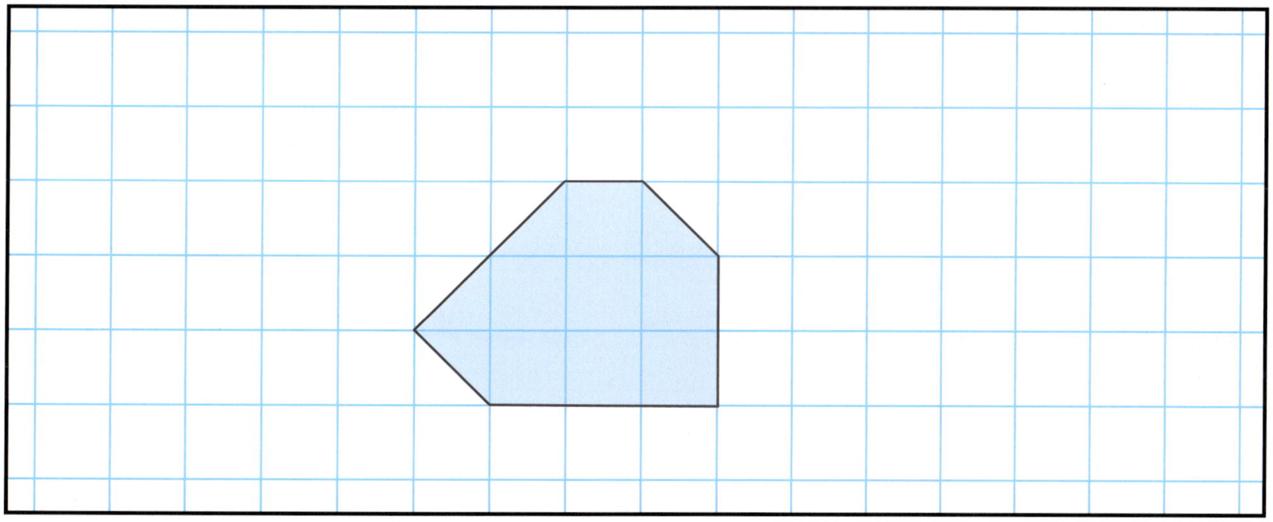

Angles

Bright sparks!

- Angles making a straight line add up to 180°.
- Angles meeting at a point add up to 360°.
- Angles in a triangle add up to 180°.

1(a) Here is the control for a shower.

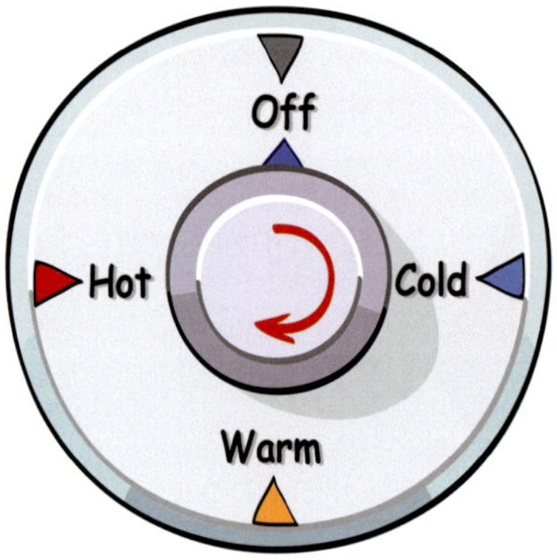

How many degrees does the pointer turn through from **off** to **cold**? [ ]°

(b) How many degrees does the pointer turn through from **cold** to **hot**? [ ]°

2 Here are some angles.

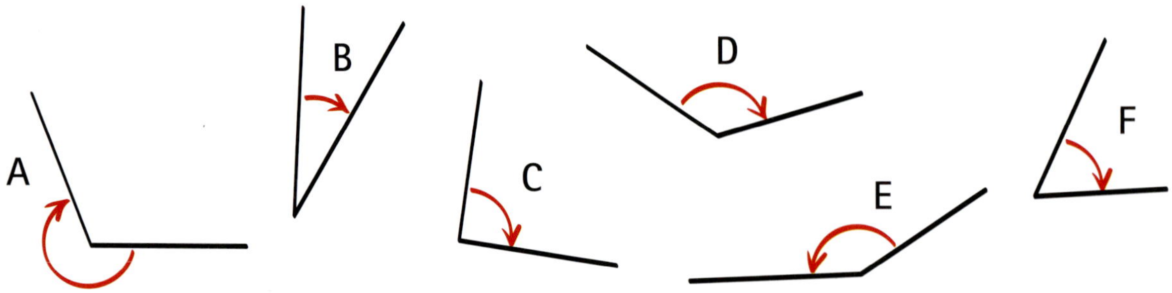

Which two of the angles are **obtuse**? [ ] and [ ]

3 Here is an **isosceles** triangle.

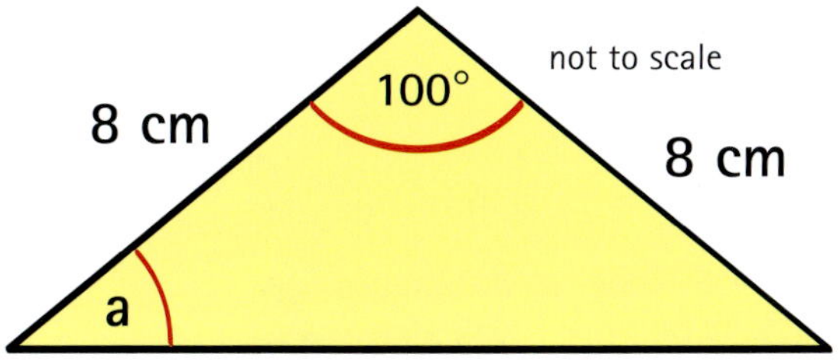

Calculate the size of angle **a**. [   ]°

(*Do* **not** *use a protractor/angle measurer.*)

Show your **working**.
You may get a mark.

4(a) Maria has drawn a rectangle.

She draws a sloping line inside it as shown.

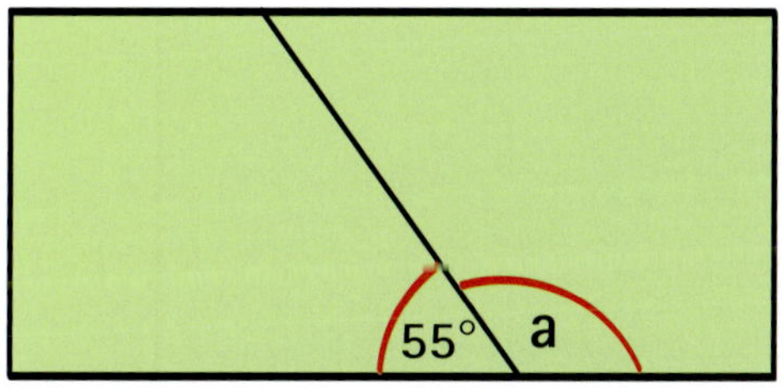

Calculate the size of **angle a**. [   ]°

(*Do* **not** *use a protractor/angle measurer.*)

(b) On the rectangle below accurately draw the sloping line at the correct angle.

(*Use a protractor/angle measurer.*)

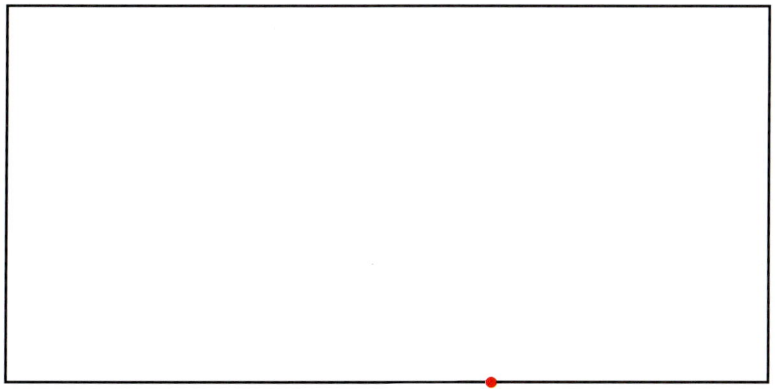

Symmetry and transformations

Bright sparks!

- A line of symmetry divides a shape so that one half is a mirror image of the other.
- A shape may have more than one line of symmetry. Some shapes have none.

1 Draw the **reflection** of the shape in the mirror line.

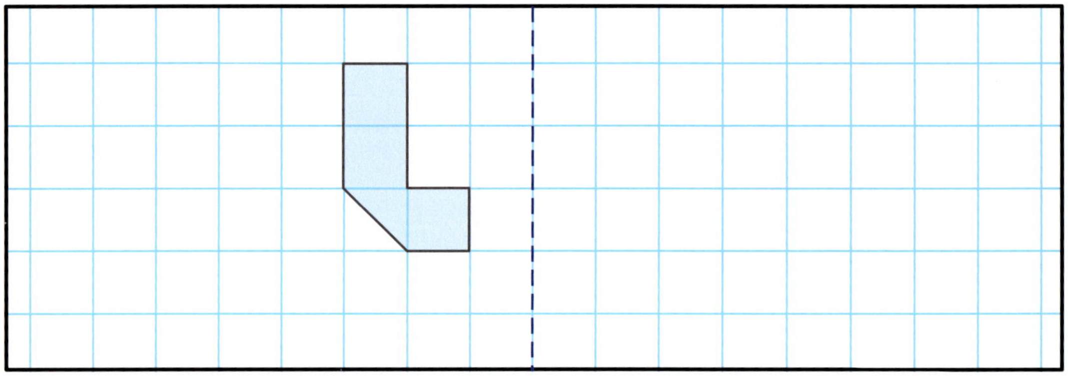

2 This **hexagon** has one line of symmetry.

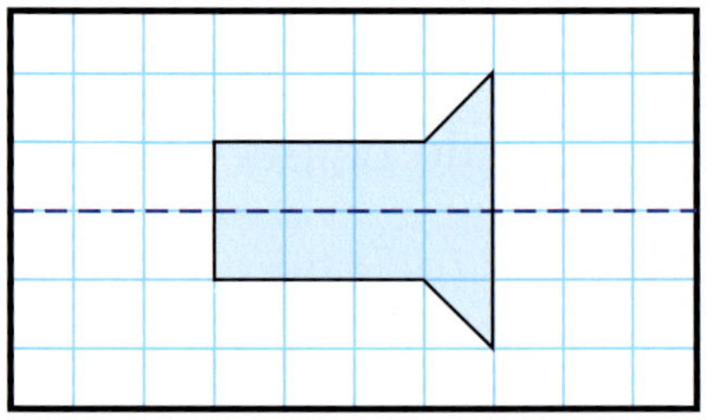

Draw a hexagon with **two** lines of symmetry.

3 Look at the shape on the grid.

Rotate the shape **90° clockwise** about C.

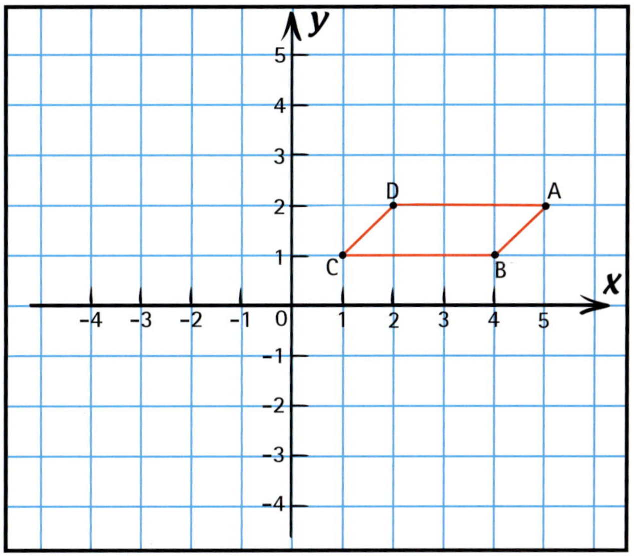

4 Complete the reflection of the pattern.

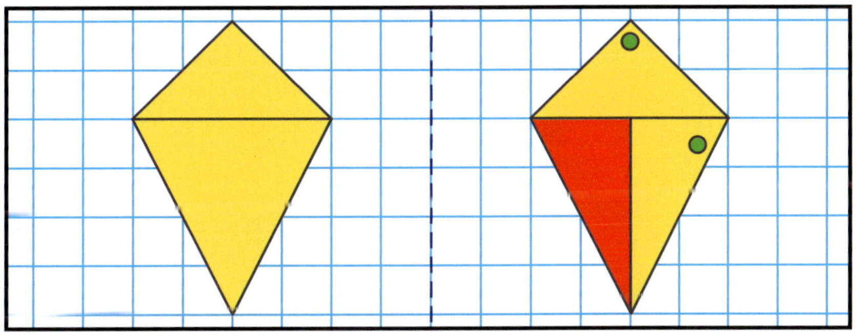

5 Shape A has been translated to shape B.
Shape A has moved 2 **squares to the left** and 3 **squares down**.

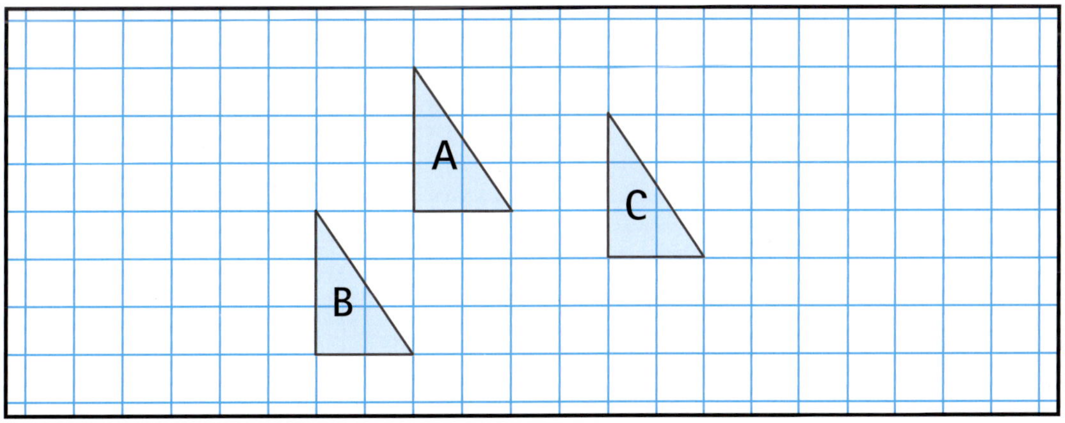

Describe the translation of **shape** A to **shape** C.

☐ squares to the ☐ and ☐ square ☐

Units and measures

Bright sparks!

- Length 1 km = 1000 m; 1 m = 100 cm; 1 cm = 10 mm
- Mass 1 kg = 1000 g
- Capacity 1 l = 1000 ml
- Time 1 week = 7 days 1 day = 24 hours
  1 hour = 60 minutes 1 minute = 60 seconds

1(a) Here are two pages from a calendar.

August

Sun		4	11	18	25
Mon		5	12	19	26
Tues		6	13	20	27
Wed		7	14	21	28
Thu	1	8	15	22	29
Fri	2	9	16	23	30
Sat	3	10	17	24	31

September

Sun	1	8	15	22	29
Mon	2	9	16	23	30
Tues	3	10	17	24	
Wed	4	11	18	25	
Thu	5	12	19	26	
Fri	6	13	20	27	
Sat	7	14	21	28	

What day is **29th August?** [ ]

(b) Tim sets off on holiday on **Friday 23rd August.**
He returns **three weeks** later on a Friday.
On which date will Tim return?

day month

(c) How many days are there between **Thursday 15th August** and **Monday 9th September**, including these two days? [ ]

2(a) Jamie is going for a run.

He starts his run at **9:35 am.**

He runs for **50 minutes.**
At what time does Jamie stop running?

(b) The next day Jamie starts his run **25 minutes earlier** and runs for **45 minutes.**

Write down the times at which Jamie started and finished his run.

Start **Finish**

3(a) Here is part of a TV programme listing.

6:00 am	Breakfast News	12:00 am	Passport to the Sun
9:00	Kilroy	12:30	Through the Keyhole
10:00	Garden Invaders	1:00	News
10:30	House Invaders	1:30	Regional News
11:00	Trading up	1:45	Neighbours
11:30	Bargain Hunt	2:10	Cagney and Lacey

How long does the **News** and **Regional News** last altogether?

(b) **Cagney and Lacey** starts at **2:10 pm.**
Write this time as it would appear on a 24-hour digital clock.

(c) Nick gets up at **7:50 am.** He watches TV for **two and a half hours,** then switches it off.

Which programme will be on TV when he switches it off?

4 Bethany knows that her rabbit weighs **1400 grams** (g).
She puts it on a set of scales which measure weight in **kilograms** (kg).

Mark with an arrow ↓ the weight of her rabbit on this scale.

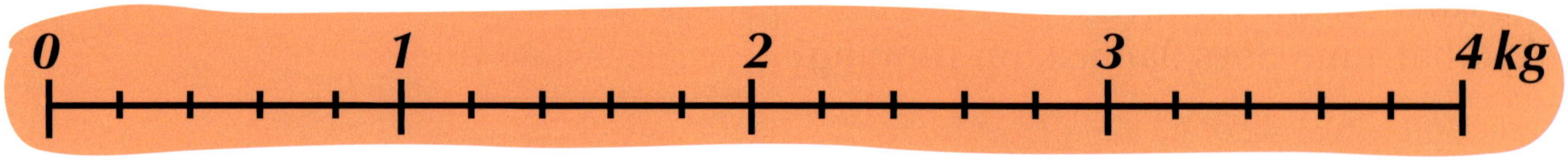

5(a) Nathan pours some milk into a jug.

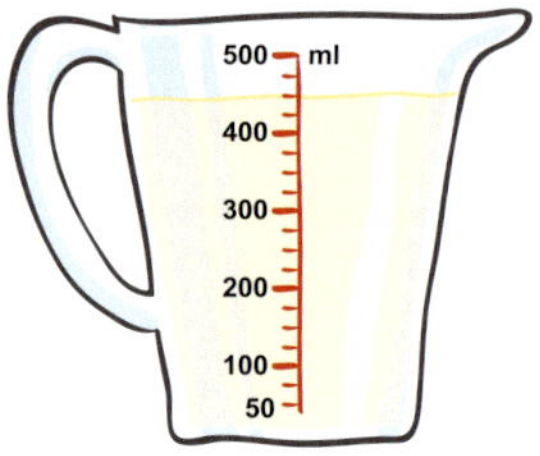

How much milk is in the jug? [ml]

(b) He pours himself a glass of milk.
The glass contains **125 ml.**

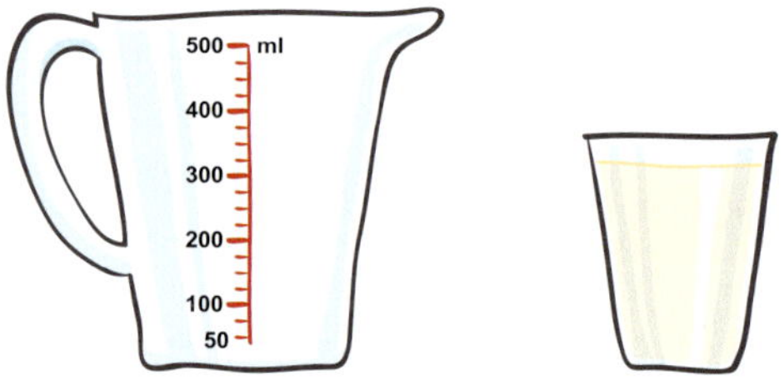

Draw an arrow ⟶ to show the level of the milk in the jug now.

6 Abram has measured the heights of three of his friends using different scales.

Write the heights of Paul and Jade in **centimetres** in the boxes.

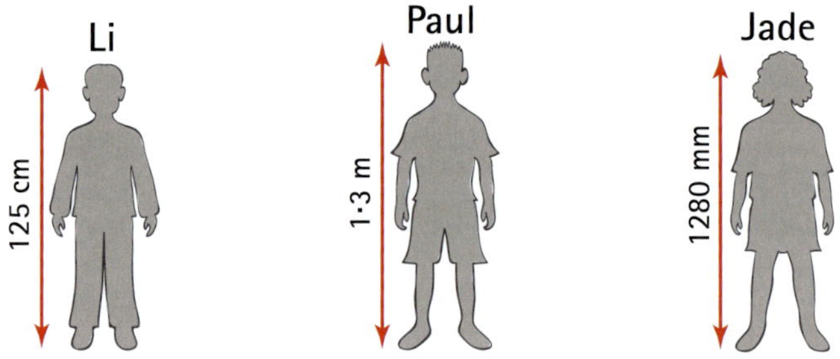

[125 cm] [cm] [cm]

7 Asha is changing some of her money from pounds (£) into euros (€).

£2 is worth approximately **3 euros.**

She receives **60 euros.** How many pounds is this? [£]

Mathematics Key Stage 2 Practice test

Instructions

You may use a calculator to answer Questions 5 and 17 only.

Work as quickly and as carefully as you can.

You have **45 minutes** for this test.

If you cannot do one of the questions, **go on to the next one.** You can come back to it later, if you have time.

If you finish before the end, **go back and check your work.**

Follow the instructions for each question carefully.

This shows where you need to put the answer.

If you need to do working out, you can use any space on a page.

Some questions look like this:

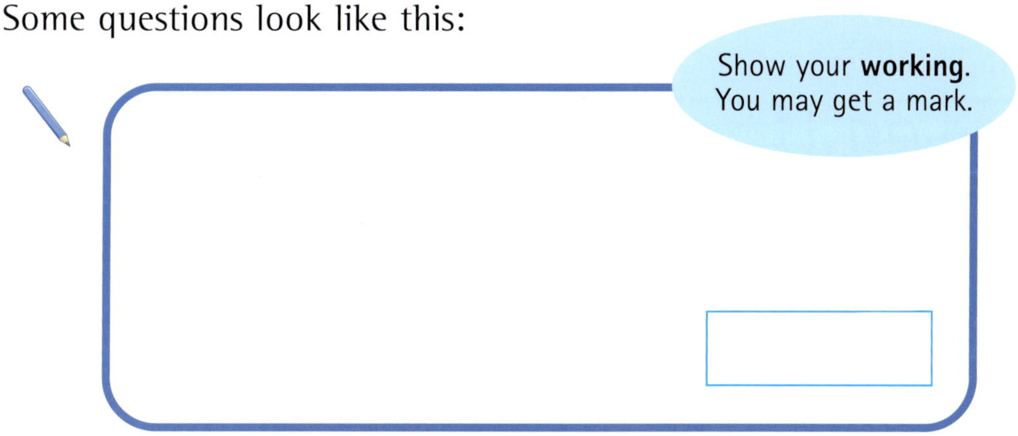

For these questions you may get a mark for showing your method.

1

(a) Here are four digits.

6 **8** **1** **5**

Use **all** the digits 6, 8, 1 and 5 to make the **smallest odd** number possible.

1a
1 mark

(b) Now use **all** the digits to make the **largest even** number possible.

1b
1 mark

2

Circle **two** numbers that have a **difference** of **70**.

40 100 130 10 60 190

2
1 mark

3

Draw lines to join clocks showing the same times.

7:00 AM	10:00 AM	7:00 PM	8:00 PM
19:00	7:00	20:00	10:00

3
1 mark

4

Olivia has drawn a **trapezium**.

Draw **one** line inside the shape to make a parallelogram and a triangle.

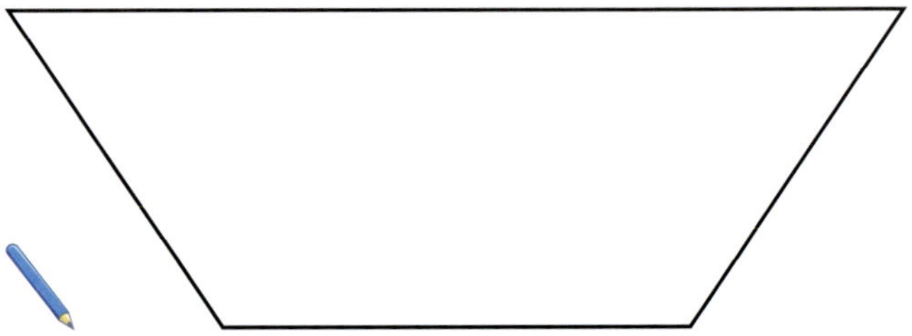

4
1 mark

5

	5 x 1·5	
3·2 x 2	6·5	32·5 ÷ 5
7·9 – 1·4		3·4 + 4·1

Draw lines from the number in the middle to the **two** boxes which have **6·5** as the answer.

(You may use a calculator.)

5 — 1 mark

6

(a) Pencils are sold in packs of 25.

How many pencils are there in **nine** packs?

6a — 1 mark

(b) Michael needs to buy **450** pencils.

How many packs would he need?

6b — 1 mark

7

Kirsty is thinking of a 2D shape.

She describes the shape to her friend Jo.

'It is a quadrilateral. It does not have any parallel sides. Both pairs of equal sides touch each other.'

What is Kirsty's shape?

7 — 1 mark

8

A group of **five** friends go bowling.

Here is the price list:

TOP TEN BOWLING

Prices per person

1 game	£2
2 games	£3.50
3 games	£5
Shoe hire	50p

The group decides to have **two** games each.

Work out the total cost for the **games** and **shoe hire** for all five friends.

Show your **working**. You may get a mark.

£

8 — 2 marks

9

Write in the missing numbers to complete the addition.

$$\begin{array}{cccc} & \square & 3 & \square \\ + & 2 & 4 & 9 \\ \hline & 5 & \square & 7 \end{array}$$

9

1 mark

10

What is $\frac{2}{5}$ of 560? ☐

10

1 mark

11

Here are some **nets**.

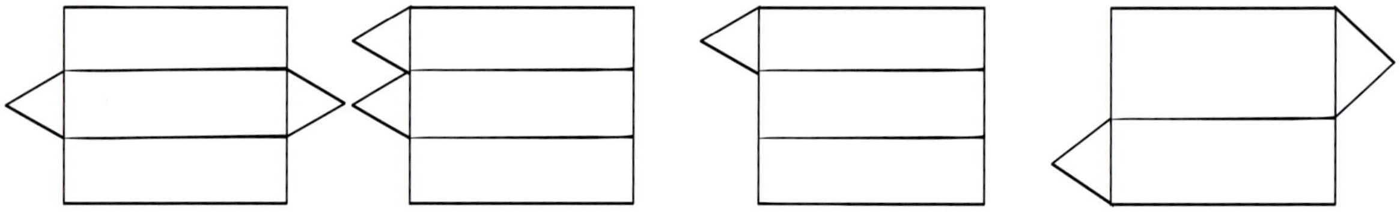

Put a tick inside the net which will fold up to make a **triangular prism.**

11

1 mark

12

Measure the diagonal of the rectangle.
Give your answer in millimetres. ☐ mm

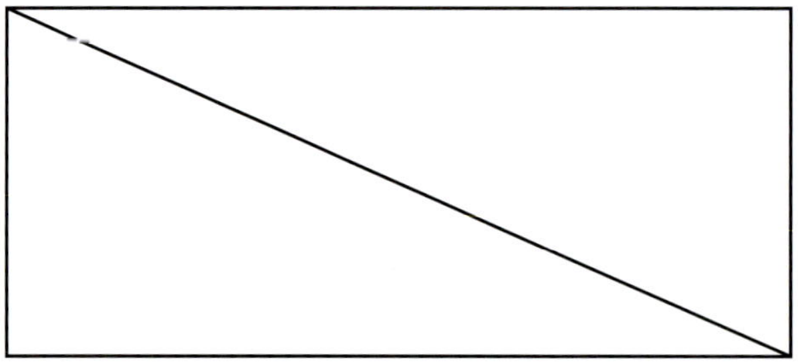

12

1 mark

13

(a) James drew a pictogram to show the number of sunny days in June, July and August.

Key:  is 4 days

Draw a **bar chart** to show the same information.

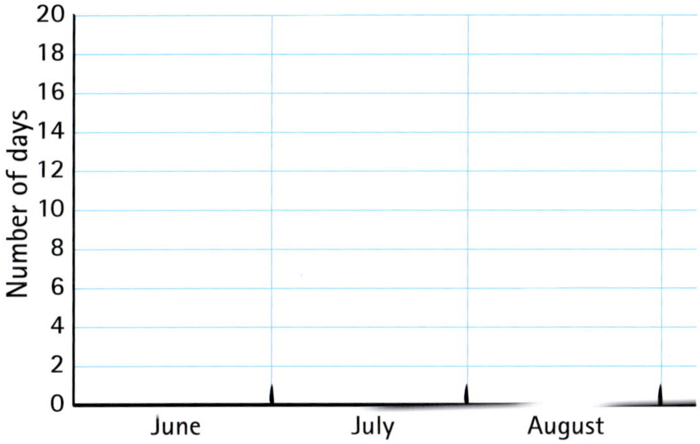

13a

1 mark

(b) How many sunny days are there altogether in June, July and August?

13b

1 mark

14

Draw circles around the **two** fractions which are equivalent to $\frac{1}{3}$.

$\frac{10}{15}$ $\frac{3}{10}$ $\frac{4}{12}$ $\frac{10}{30}$ $\frac{4}{6}$

14

1 mark

15

Here are two thermometers.

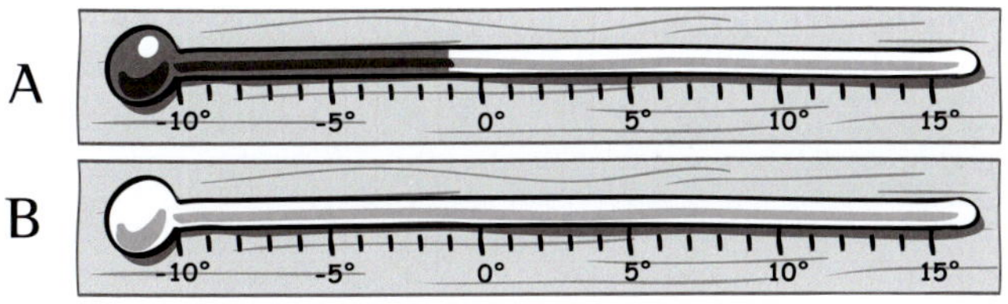

(a) What is the temperature on **thermometer** A?

15a

1 mark

(b) Mark the temperature -6°C on thermometer B.

15b

1 mark

16

16 — 2 marks

Complete the table.

One row has been done for you.

Number	Rounded to nearest ten	Rounded to nearest hundred
123	120	100
255		
92·7		

17

17 — 1 mark

Calculate **15% of £1560.**

(You **may** *use a calculator.)*

18

18a — 1 mark

(a) Hojin rolls a 1-6 dice.

What is the probability of Hojin rolling the number 6 on the dice?
Give your answer as a **fraction.**

(b) Hojin says, **'There is an even chance of rolling an odd number on the dice.'**

Is he correct?

Circle Yes or No. **Yes / No**

Explain your answer.

18b — 1 mark

19

19 — 1 mark

Write in the missing numbers in this sequence.

☐ 10 20 40 ☐ 160

20

Calculate 284 x 23.

Show your **working**. You may get a mark.

20 — 2 marks

21

(a) Here is a tiled floor.

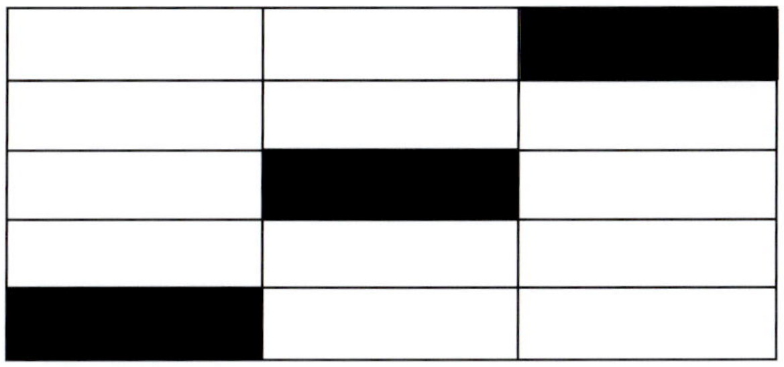

What is the ratio of black tiles to white tiles? [:]

21a — 1 mark

(b) What is the proportion of black tiles?
Give your answer as a **fraction**.

21b — 1 mark

22

Some capital letters have lines of reflective symmetry.

Look at the letters below:

The letter A has **one** line of symmetry.

Put the letters in the correct boxes. The letter A has been done for you.

No lines of symmetry	One line of symmetry	More than one line of symmetry
	A	

22 — 2 marks

23

(a) Here is a grid.

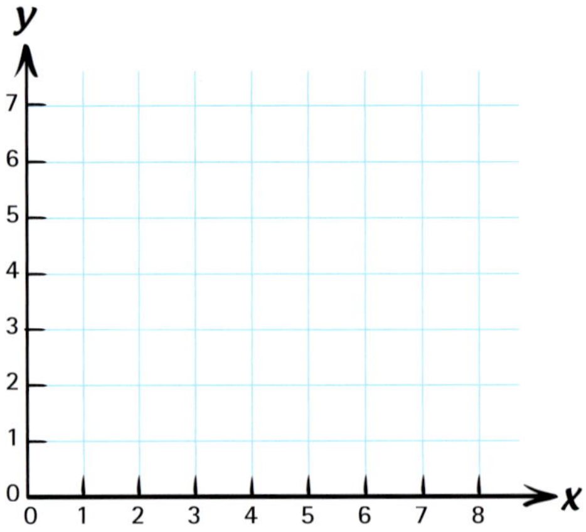

Plot the points.

A (2, 1)

B (6, 1)

C (4, 7)

23a

1 mark

Join your points to form a **triangle**.

(b) Which word best describes this triangle?

Tick **one** box.

isosceles ☐ scalene ☐ equilateral ☐ right-angled ☐

23b

1 mark

24

Bob cuts one slice from a whole pizza.

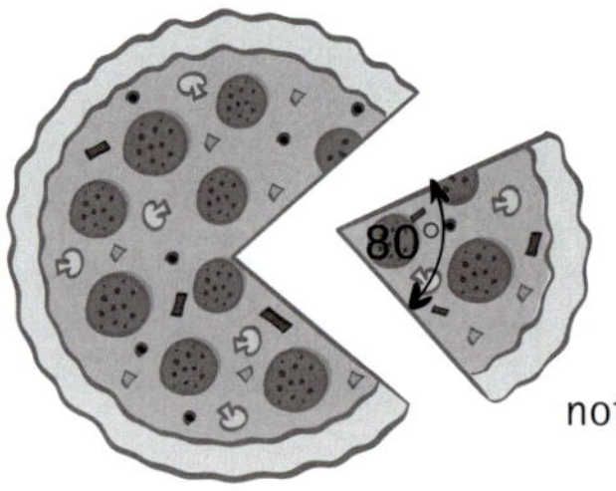

not to scale

Bob cuts a second slice for his friend Joe.
A picture of the remaining pizza is shown below.

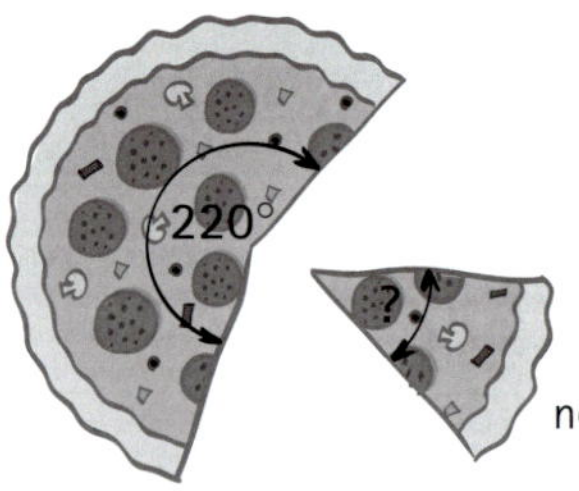

not to scale

Show your **working**.
You may get a mark.

Work out, **in degrees**, the size of Joe's slice of pizza.

°

24

2 marks

25

(a) Here are two multiplication facts.

$4 \times 78 = 312$

$13 \times 78 = 1014$

Show how Jamilla can use these two facts to work out **17 x 78.**

....

....

25a
1 mark

(b) What is **40** x **78**? [ ]

25b
1 mark

26

(a) Here are some shapes in a grid.

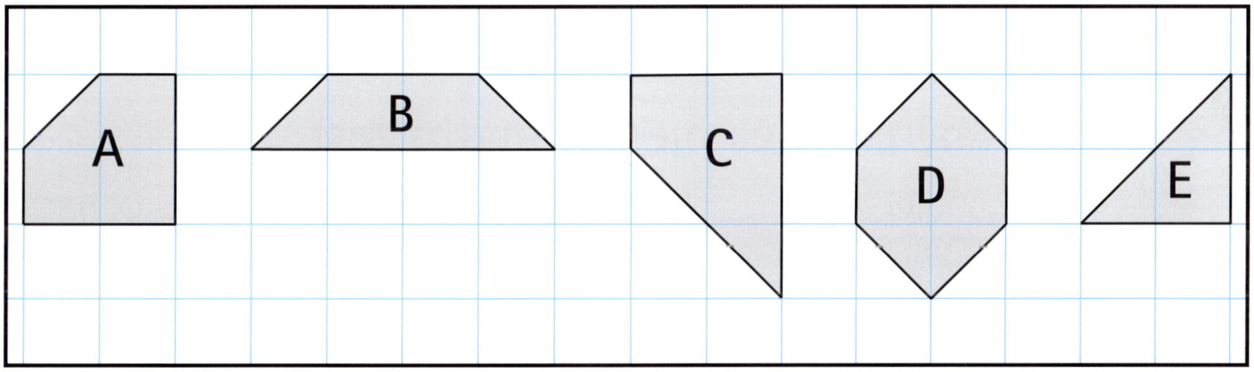

Which **two** shapes have an **equal area**?

[ ] and [ ]

26a
1 mark

(b) Which **two** shapes have an **equal perimeter**?

[ ] and [ ]

Total (*40 marks*)

26b
1 mark

Mental maths test

About the mental test

In school the mental test is played on a cassette. The tape starts with some instructions about the test for the children. After this introduction the tape is stopped so that they can ask the teacher any questions if necessary. The children are not allowed to ask further questions once the tape has been restarted.

There are 20 questions of varying degrees of difficulty, each worth one mark. Each question is read out twice and a certain amount of time is allowed for your child to work out and write down an answer. An answer box is provided for each question. The answer must be written in this box. Working out should be done mentally but, if necessary, your child can make jottings outside the box. There is no need to show working out as it does not gain any more marks and in some cases can lead your child to miss the next question. Next to some questions information is provided, e.g. numbers, diagrams, shapes, for which your child will need to work out an answer.

Practice mental maths test

- Photocopy the next page. Cut the sheet in two where shown. The left-hand section is for you to read out to your child. The right-hand section forms the answer grid for your child.
- Choose a good time for the test and find a quiet room where you will not be disturbed.
- Explain the instructions, as outlined above, to your child.
- Read out each question twice. Allow your child five seconds to answer each of questions 1 to 5, 10 seconds for each of questions 6 to 15, and 15 seconds for each of questions 16 to 20.

Answers to the practice mental maths test

1	10:20	Only accept a numerical answer.
2	150 seconds	2 x 60 + 30 = 150.
3	740	735 is exactly half way between 730 and 740 so round up to 740.
4	8°C	Do not accept any other answer.
5	45	A good method is to double 20, add 7, then take away 2.
6	11·1	Add 7 and 3 to get 10, then add the tenths.
7	first angle	Obtuse angles are greater than 90° but less than 180°.
8	7:10 or 10 past 7	Allow an answer in a different format provided it is the correct time.
9	$\frac{2}{10}$ or $\frac{1}{5}$ or 20%	2 out of 10 are red but the answer must be a fraction or a percentage.
10	28	Work out 32 - 24, halve, then add to 24, or halve the total of 24 and 32.
11	both 12 and 36	Multiples are 'answers to times tables'.
12	8 cm	Take away the two shorter sides to leave 16 cm, then divide by 2.
13	96 pence	26 + 2 x 35 = 26 + 70 = 96.
14	52	A subtraction is needed here, 68 - 16 = 52.
15	6030	Notice that there are no hundreds so use a zero in that column.
16	£6	Divide by 10 to get 10%, then halve it to get 5%.
17	116 degrees	Angles on a straight line add up to 180°. Work out 180 – 64.
18	9	The chart is marked in eighths, each worth 3 (24/8), then 3 x 3 = 9.
19	0·07	0·07 has no tenths so is the smallest.
20	9 cm^2	Accept answers between 8·5 and 9·5 cm^2

1 The time is twenty past ten in the morning. What time would a digital clock show?

2 How many seconds are there in two and a half minutes?

3 Round the number 735 to the nearest ten.

4 What is the reading on the thermometer?

5 Double 19 and then add 7.

6 What is 7·3 added to 3·8?

7 Put a ring around the obtuse angle.

8 A bus arrives at the station at 7:45. It is 35 minutes late. At what time should it have arrived?

9 A bag contains 6 white balls, 2 red balls and 2 green balls. What is the probability of picking a red ball?

10 Which number is half way between 24 and 32?

11 Put rings around the numbers which are multiples of 12.

12 The perimeter of a rectangle is 24 cm. Its shorter sides are each 4 cm. What is the length of one of its longer sides?

13 A ruler costs 26 pence and a pencil costs 35 pence. How much would two pencils and a ruler cost altogether?

14 If 16 is added to a number the answer is 68. What is the number?

15 Write the number six thousand and thirty in figures.

16 What is 5% of £120?

17 What is the size of the angle marked with the letter **a** in the diagram?

18 The pie chart shows the favourite colour of 24 children. How many children like blue?

19 Put a ring around the smallest number.

20 What is the approximate area of the shape on the grid?

1 [:]

2 seconds

3 735

4 °C

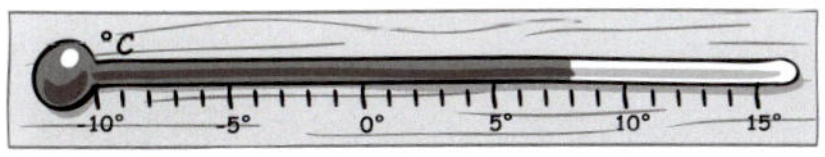

5 19 7

6 7·3 3·8

7

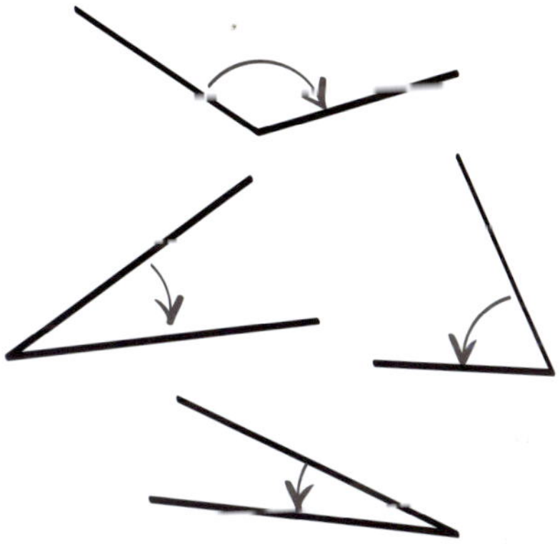

8 7:45

9

10 24 32

11 4 6 12 16 36 71

12 cm 24 cm 4 cm

13 26p 35p

14 16 68

15

16 £ £120 5%

17 °

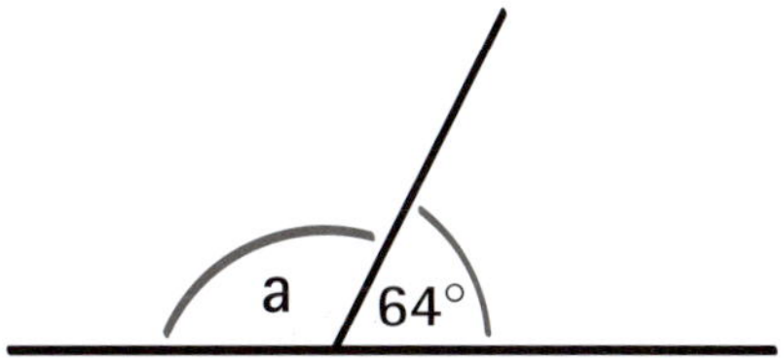

18

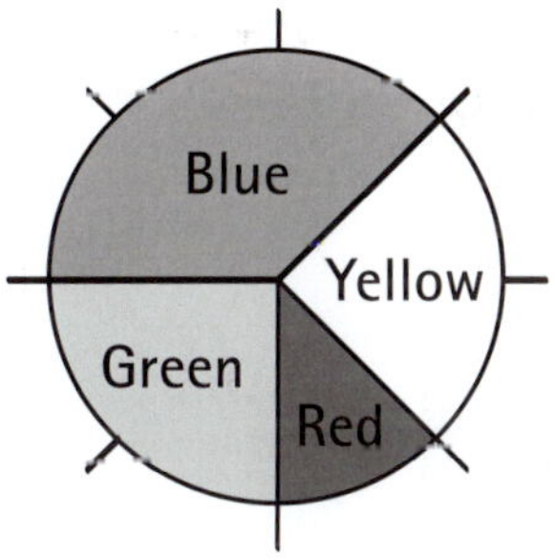

19 0·7 0·07 0·17 0·69 0·1

20 cm²

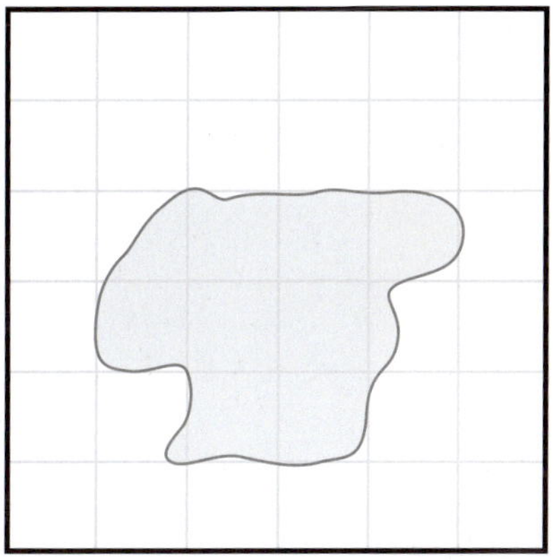

Sample test questions and answers

Here are three questions selected from past National Tests. These questions were chosen to give an insight into the way questions are actually marked and the errors that children tend to make.

2002 Test A, Question 11

Mr Singh buys paving slabs to go around his pond.

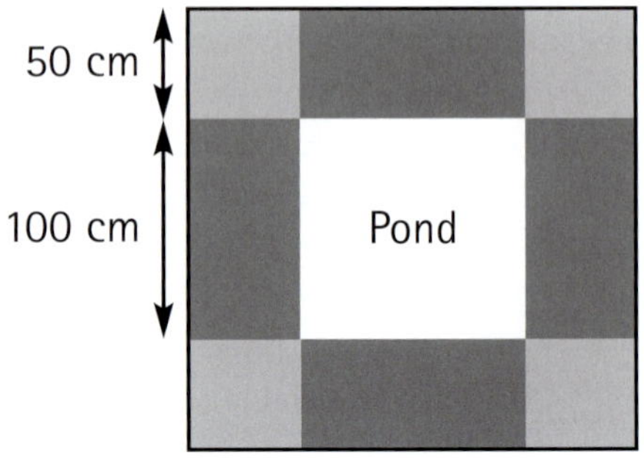

PAVING SLABS

£1.95 each	Square slabs 50 cm by 50 cm
£3.50 each	Rectangular slabs 100 cm by 50 cm

He buys 4 rectangular slabs and 4 square slabs.

What is the total cost of the slabs he buys?

Show your **working**. You may get a mark.

Mr Singh says, **'It would cost more to use square slabs all the way round.'**

Explain why he is correct.

This question asks your child to show working. A mark may be awarded where sufficient correct working out has been done but the final answer is incorrect.

Two marks would be awarded for giving one of the following answers: £21.80, £21.80p, £21 80. Only one mark would be awarded for answers of £2180p, £2180 or £21.8. Where the final answer is incorrect, a mark may be given for the following:

£3.50 x 4 = £14.00
£1.95 x 4 = £7.80
£14.00 + £7.80 = wrong answer

In the second part of the question your child is asked to show an understanding that each square slab costs more than half a rectangular one.

Acceptable answers include 'half of £3.50 (cost of rectangular slab) is £1.75 and a square slab costs £1.95', 'two square slabs cost more than one rectangular slab', 'twelve square slabs cost £23.40' or 'it would cost £1.60 more'.
Vague answers such as 'he would need more slabs', 'square slabs are cheaper', 'it costs more' or repeating part of the question would not score a mark.

2002 Test B, Question 5

Use a ruler to draw one line of symmetry on each of these designs.

You may use a mirror or tracing paper.

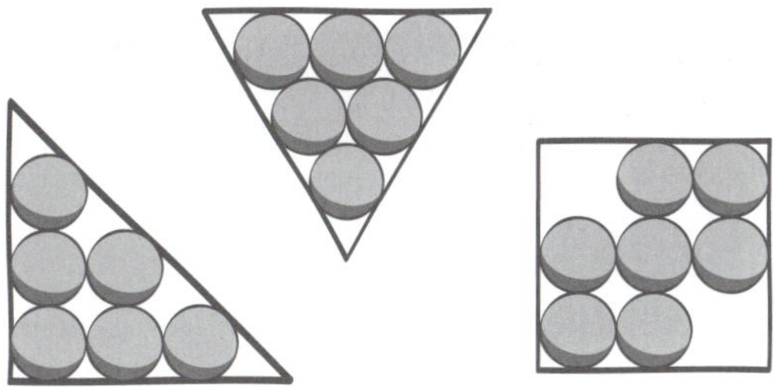

This question is about reflective symmetry. Your child would be provided with both tracing paper and a mirror for use in this question.

Two marks would be awarded for all three correct and one mark for any two correct. The correct lines are shown below. Note that only one line on each is needed.

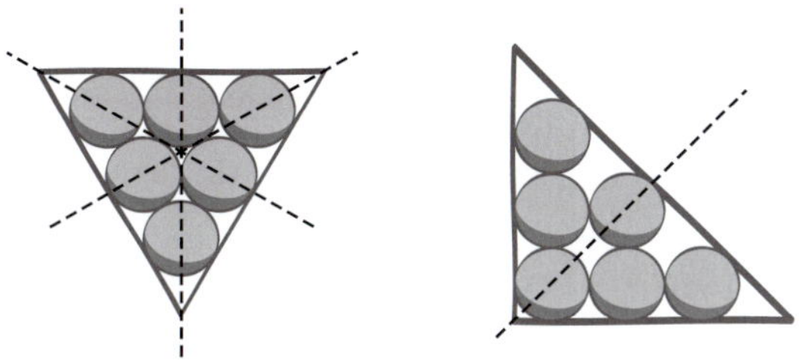

Your child would not lose marks if the lines are slightly inaccurate or not drawn with a ruler, or if more than one line of symmetry is drawn, provided all the lines drawn are correct. The length of the line is unimportant provided the intention is clear.

2001 Test A, Question 25

This is a centimetre grid.

Draw 3 **more lines** to make a **parallelogram** with an **area of 10 cm²**.

Use a ruler.

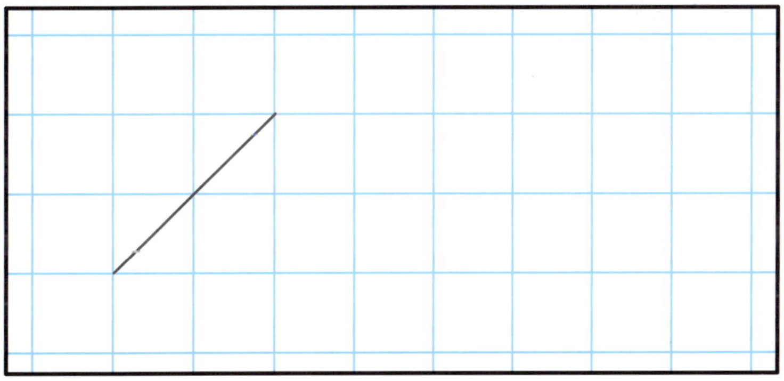

This question at first appears easy but many children may find it difficult to achieve both the correct shape and area at the same time.

A good method would be to sketch a parallelogram first to keep in mind the shape to be drawn. Then use a pencil and eraser to sketch lines on the grid until a parallelogram is drawn with the correct area. Slight inaccuracies are ignored.

The most obvious shape is (a) but various others are possible (e.g. b, c).

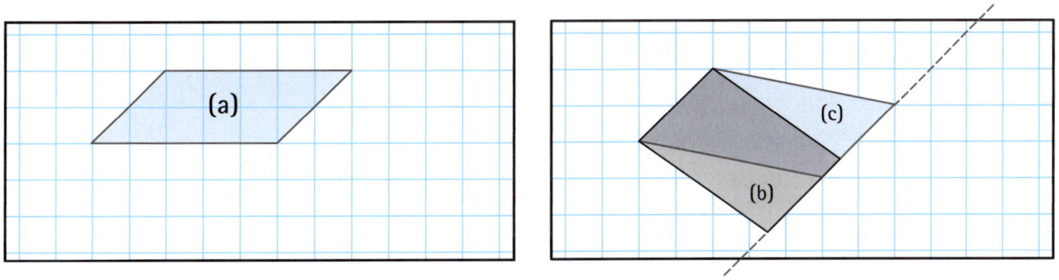

Answers to practice questions

Place value

1 (a) 9841 (b) 1984

2 0·49

3 four thousand, three hundred and eight

4

5 136 < 160, 1121 > 1112, 0·02 < 0·1

Number calculations

1 60 42 divided by 7 is 6, so 420 divided by 7 is 60

2 157

3 5·84 The question is written in a line. Encourage your child to set the question out in columns to make working out easier.

4 There are many possible correct answers. The easiest pairs are, for example, 200 - 101, 300 - 201 or 199 - 100, 299 - 200, etc.

5 Double 32 and 8 x 8 (64);
9 x 7 and 45 + 18 (63);
99 - 46 and (5 x 9) + 8 (53)

6 12 The division in the brackets must be worked out first.

7 (a) 5 weeks After 4 weeks he will only have £14, after 5 he will have exceeded £15.
(b) £4.20 Work out 10% by dividing by 10 to get 35p then double to get 20% as 70p and add to £3.50.

8 (a) £1.26 Also accept 126p. (b) 12 minutes

9 (a) 75p Also accept £0.75.
(b) £4.40 or 440p

10 48 Work out 32 + 140 then subtract the answer from 220.

11 96 + 75 or 95 + 76 (171) The highest sum is achieved by putting the higher digits in the tens columns.

12 7 x 7 x 5 Since the answer ends in 5, one of the single digit numbers must be 5. Divide 245 by 5 to give 49. The only pair of single digit numbers which multiply to give 49 are 7 and 7.

13 (a) £12 (b) £12 (c) 8

14 162 (bottom row), 159 (middle left), 191 (middle right) Work out 500 - (208 + 130) to get 162, then use a similar method for the other two sides.

Properties of numbers and sequences

1 2, 13, 21, 18.

2 (a) 9, 21, 15, 30 The numbers in the intersection must also be included.
(b) 35 is a multiple of both 3 and 5.
(c) 105, 120, 135... etc.

3 1, -3.

4 (a) 720 (b) Yes. All of the numbers in the sequence are multiples of 60. Since 3800 does not divide exactly by 60 it is not a multiple of 60 so will not appear in the sequence.

5 39, 45 Work out 51 - 33 to get 18, then divide by three to work out that the numbers increase by 6 each time.

Fractions and percentages

1 $\frac{1}{5}$, $\frac{3}{8}$, $\frac{3}{4}$, $\frac{4}{5}$. (All 4 should be in the correct order.)

2 15 Work out 35 divided by 7, then multiply by 4 to get 20 for the number of boys. 15 must be girls.

3 $\frac{3}{10}$ or $\frac{30}{100}$

4 $\frac{11}{5}$ kg or $2\frac{1}{5}$ kg

5 $\frac{4}{8}$, $\frac{1}{8}$

6 first and fourth shapes.

7

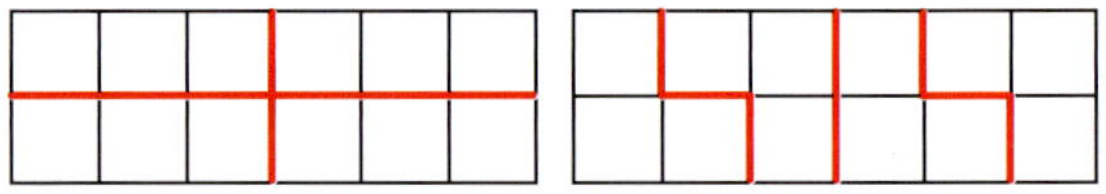

8 66p, 88p, £1.32

9 Shade any 24 squares The grid has 40 squares so 4 squares is 10%, 24 squares is 60%.

10 (a) 58% (b) 30 40% represents 12, so 10% represents 3 (12 divided by 4). 100% must therefore be 10 x 3 = 30.

Ratio and proportion

1 (a) 75 grams
(b) Yes should be circled and a correct explanation given, such as: The ratio indicates twice as much butter as sugar. There is 100 grams of butter which is twice as much as 50 grams of sugar.

2 10 35 divided by (5+2) is 5. Two packets out of every 7, so 2 x 5 = 10.

Negative numbers

1 (a) Sydney (b) 11°C

2 1 and -3

3 (a) 7°C (b) -5°C

Handling data

1 (a) 25 (b) 25 (c) £44.80 or 4480p
(20 + 25 + 40 + 40 +15) x £0.32

2 (a) ruler (b) 1

3 11, 12 or 13 Slightly more than one quarter (which is 10 children).

4 (a) 60 km (b) 2 hours
(c) He stopped because his distance did not increase over this hour.

5 (a) 0 - 3, 1 - 1, 2 - 4, 3 - 2, 4 - 1, 5 – 1
(b) 2 2 goals occurs 4 times
(c) 2 Total of 24 divided by 12 = 2

Probability

1 (a) There are more 2s than 3s so it is more likely to land on a 2.
OR There would have to be an equal number of 2s and 3s for there to be an even chance.
(b) $\frac{4}{6}$ or $\frac{2}{3}$. The answer must be a fraction.
(c) There should be more 4s than any other number on the spinner.

2 (a) $\frac{1}{12}$ (b) $\frac{6}{12}$ or $\frac{1}{2}$ or other equivalent

3 (a) 7 (b) There are more (six) ways to score 7 than any other score.
(c) 2, 12

2D and 3D shapes

1
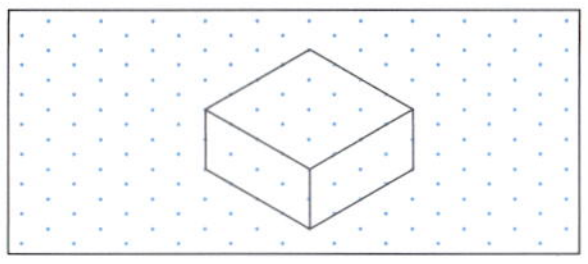

2 C, A

3
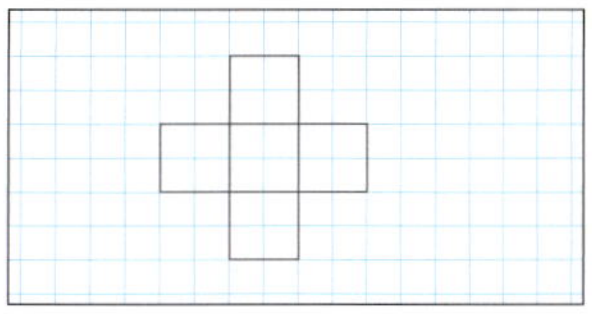

4 A – one pair of parallel sides, more than 4 sides; B – no parallel sides, more than 4 sides

5 (a) fourth shape
(b) third statement

Position and direction

1 (a) Side ED should be marked in some way.
(b) (35, 8)

2 Fastwick

3 (8, 4) The x coordinate is halfway between 4 and 12; the y coordinate is 8 below 12.

Perimeter and area

1
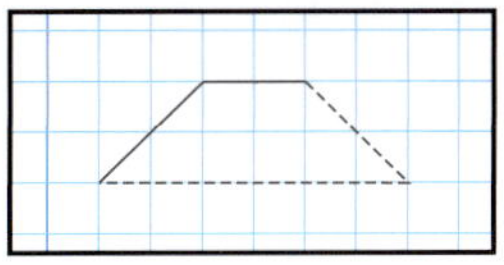
or
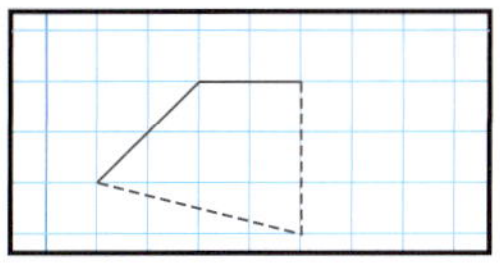

2 (a) 32 cm 12 + 12 + 4 + 4
(b) 48 cm² length x breadth, 12 x 4

3 8 cm 16 + 16 = 32, then 48 - 32 = 16, then $\frac{16}{2}$ = 8

4 10·5

5 42 cm 6 sides each of 7cm

6 9 cm² 3 squares by 3 squares

Angles

1 (a) 90° (b) 180°

2 D and E

3 40° 180 - 100 = 80 then $\frac{80}{2}$ = 40

4 (a) 125° 180 – 55
(b) check angle with protractor (A mark would be awarded if the angle is within the range 124° - 126°.)

Symmetry and transformations

1
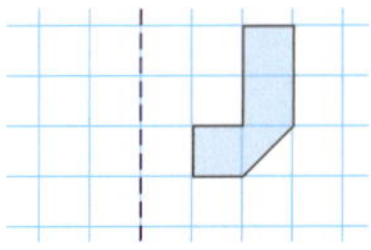

2
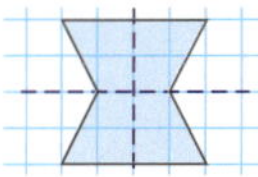
or
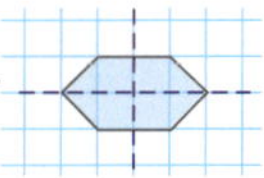

3
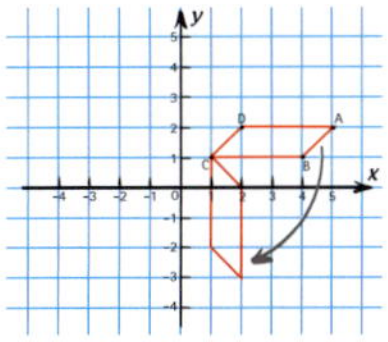

4
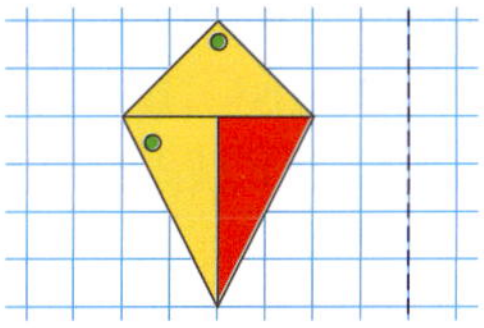

5 4 squares to the **right** and **1** square **down**.
(All 4 must be correct.)

Units and measures

1 (a) Thursday (b) 13 September
(c) 26 days

2 (a) 10:25 am or an equivalent time in words
(b) 9:10 am, 9:55 am or equivalents

3 (a) 45 minutes
(b) 1410 or 14:10 add 12 to the pm hours
(c) Garden Invaders

4 The arrow should indicate the second mark along from 1 kg – each division is 200 g or 0.2 kg.

5 (a) 450 ml (b) Arrow or line drawn across the jug indicating 325 ml (450 -125 ml).

6 Paul – 130 cm; Jade – 128 cm

7 £40 $\frac{60}{3}$ = 20 then 20 x 2 = 40

Answers to practice test

1 (a) 1685 (b) 8516

2 130 and 60

3 7:00 am - 0700; 10:00 am - 1000; 7:00 pm - 1900; 8:00 pm – 2000
(All 4 pairs must be correct to gain the mark.)

4

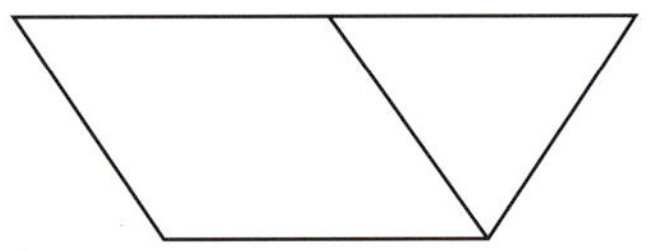

5 7·9 - 1·4 and 32·5 ÷ 5
(Both must be indicated to gain the mark.)

6 (a) 225 (b) 18

7 kite

8 £20 5 x £3.50 = £17.50 and 5 x £0.50 = £2.50 then £17.50 + £2.50 = £20.00
(or £3.50 + £0.50 = £4 then x 5 to get £20)
(Award 1 mark for showing correct method with one numerical error or for only cost of games without shoe hire given.)

9 338 + 249 = 587 (All 3 missing digits must be correct to gain the mark.)

10 224 divide 560 by 5 then x 2

11 first net

12 85 mm (Award the mark if the answer is between 84 mm and 86 mm.)

13 (a) Bars showing: June 14, July 11, August 16
(b) 41 (Award the mark only if all 3 are correct.)

14 $\frac{4}{12}$ and $\frac{10}{30}$ (Both must be correct to gain the mark.)

15 (a) –1
(b)

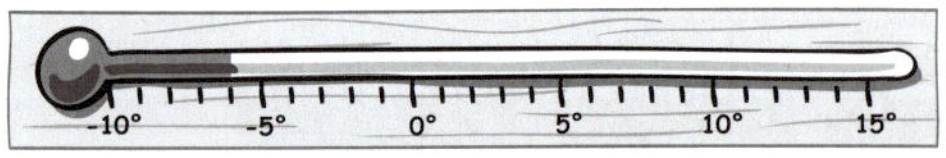

16 255 – 260, 300, 92·7 – 90, 100 (Award 1 mark for any 2 answers correct, and both marks for all correct.)

17 £234

18 (a) $\frac{1}{6}$ (b) Yes Answers should explain that there is an equal number (3 of each) of odd and even numbers on the dice. ('Yes', and correct explanation needed to gain the mark.)

19 5, 80 The number is doubled or multiplied by 2 to get the next number. (Both numbers are needed for the mark.)

20 6532 (Award one mark for any correct method with one numerical error.)

21 (a) 3:12 or 1:4 (b) $\frac{3}{15}$ or $\frac{1}{5}$

22 no lines – S, 1 line – C, M, more than 1 line – H, X, O (Award 1 mark for any 3 correct, 2 marks for all correct.)

23 (a) All three points must be correct for the mark
(b) isosceles

24 60° 360 - 80 = 280 then 280 - 220 = 60; or 80 + 220 = 300 then 360 - 300 = 60 (Award one mark for an incorrect answer but where a method attempting to subtract from 360 is shown.)

25 (a) Either show the calculation 1014 + 312 = 1326 or explain that 13 lots and 4 lots of 78 will give 17 lots of 78.
(b) 3120

26 (a) C and D (b) B and C (For each part, both answers must be correct to gain the mark.)

Awarding a level for the practice test and mental test

There are 40 possible marks on the practice test and 20 on the mental test. Double the score from the practice test and add it to the score for the mental test. Compare this final score with the figures in the table below and read off the corresponding level. The marks required for each level are approximately based on those used to determine levels in the KS2 National Tests. Most pupils are expected to achieve Level 4 in the National Tests.

Level	Score
N	17 or less
2	18-20
3	21-50
4	51-80
5	81-100